The Hybrid

Carla Kingsley

Copyright © 2024 by CARLA KINGSLEY

All rights reserved.

No portion of this book may be reproduced in any form without written permission from the publisher or author, except as permitted by U.S. copyright law.

Contents

1. ~prologue~ — 1
2. ~chapter 1~ — 2
3. ~chapter 2~ — 8
4. ~chapter 3~ — 15
5. ~chapter 4~ — 20
6. -chapter 5- — 25
7. -chapter 6- — 30
8. -chapter 7- — 34
9. -chapter 8- — 42
10. -chapter 9- — 48
11. -chapter 10- — 54
12. -chapter 11- — 59
13. -chapter 12- — 64
14. -chapter 13- — 69
15. -chapter 14- — 75

16. -chapter 15- 82

17. -chapter 16- 88

18. -chapter 17- 95

19. -chapter 18- 100

20. -chapter 19- 107

21. -chapter 20- 115

22. -chapter 21- 123

~prologue~

All I wanted was a normal life. I am chased down by people who think I am too powerful. I am beaten and tortured when they find out who I am or more importantly what I am. I try to hide it but sometimes people find out and I have to move again. This is the fifth time I have had to move in the past two years. The only difference is that I am actually starting on the first day and not in the middle of the semester. My mom moves me immediately when someone finds out or even if they have a little suspicion. I try to make friends but that always back fires. I try to hide who I am but that is harder than it looks. Now I am moving to a small town in Louisiana hoping not to get caught it or to be accepted of who I really am.

Don't steal my story. Okay thanks. :)

~chapter 1~

Okay I can do this.

I have done this before.

Fifth time is the charm.

I just parked my car in front of the new school. I mean I was nervous even though this is my fifth time doing this in the last two years.

I should probably introduce myself since you are following me around and looking at my life. My name is Bailey Wild. I have light brown hair that goes down my back. I have red eyes but I have to cover them with green color contacts so people don't find out what I am. I am average height but I would like to be taller so I can reach stuff easier but life's unfair like that. Anyway this is the fifth time I have had to move in the past two years because shit happens. The difference about this time is that I am actually starting on the first day of school. I am happy about that because that means there could be other new students so people can pay attention to them and not me. Anyway that's my life and now let's go back to the parking lot where I am deciding wether to go or not.

"You can do it Bailey. Just open the door and walk to the front of the school and walk in." I said to give me a burst of encouragement. I slowly opened the door to my 2012 Hyundai Elantra and got out. I walked to the front of the school and opened the door and walked in. I looked around to see that there was tables lined against the wall with people sitting at them handing students there stuff. I looked around and saw that it was organized by grade level. I went down the hall a little and got to the table labeled Juniors. I got into line and waited for the people in front of me to move up. Right when I was about to be first I felt something hot hit my back. "Ow." I said because it was scorching hot."Oh my gosh I am so sorry!" The girl said. "The idiots behind me where pushing each other and they pushed me into you." She said she started wiping the back of my shirt but I smelt coffee so I know that it won't come out."It's okay I have another shirt I can change into." I said starting to feel the stickiness from the coffee getting on my back."I'm Ashley by the way." She said holding her hand out."Hi I'm Bailey. I'm new." I said and then the scent hit me. Mermaid. I looked at the girl and she was smiling and I noticed that she does look like a mermaid with blonde hair and blue eyes."No wonder I didn't recognize your face. I am head of student council and head cheerleader so I should know everybody." She said. She wasn't one of those stereotypical cheerleader who dressed like a slut and was a bitch. She was actually pretty nice."Oh well now you know everybody." I said with a chuckle."Yeah it is hard to remember but since it's a small school it isn't impossible.""Excuse me can you come get your schedule?" The lady who was sitting behind the desk said a little rudely."Sorry." I said and walked up."Bailey Wild.""Bailey Wild." She flipped through the papers until she got to mine and handed to me."Thank you." I said and walked away."Bailey!" I heard someone shout. I turned around and Ashley was walking towards me with her schedule in her hands."Here let's see if we have any classes together." She took my schedule and analyzed while I just awkwardly stood there waiting for her to finish. "We have first and second period together and also last.""Awesome do you mind showing me to my first hour since I kinda don't know where I am going." I said with a shy smile.She chuckled. "Sure."

::

It wasn't long before we walked into my first hour class. I made sure to memorize where we were going so I wouldn't get lost."Now don't talk in this class unless you have a death wish." Ashley said."Miss Menard is a bitch when she needs to be." Ashley said.We walked in and we sat in the middle of the class since no one was really there yet. "So what brings you to Louisiana?" Ashley said turning towards me."Family issues." I said with a shrug. I would have said personal issues but I don't want her to ask questions. "Ahh I have family issues too with my mom. She can be a bitch sometimes.""It is really on my mom's part she can be a bit over protective of me." I said with a sad smile." I mean I love my mom but she can give me some space you know?""That sounds awesome my mom barely cares where I am or what I do. I feel like I am not even her daughter sometimes.""Maybe she is just giving you tough love?" I suggested."No because she gives my twin brother more attention than me." She said with a shrug. "That sucks I'm sorry about that.""Don't be sorry about it. I don't want your pity." She said."Okay.""Hey babe." Some really hot dude that sat next to Ashley said. He had a really deep voice that made shivers go up my spine."Hey Jason." Ashley said kissing his cheek."Who is this?" Jason said nodding his head towards me."Bailey. She's new here." Ashley said giving me a smile."Hi." I said shyly. "Nice to meet you.""You too. Where you moved here from?" He asked."From-" I got caught off when the teacher walked in. She looked like she was in her 50's she had blonde hair and brown eyes and was short and looked like she worked out."My name is Miss Menard. I will be your science teacher for this year. Today we-" she got cut off by someone opening the door and walking in. He was tall. Then it hit me. Vampire."That's Mark he is always late and you don't want to get on his bad side." Ashley whispered in my ear. Don't worry I won't."Nice for you to join us Mark. Now go take a seat."

The rest of the class period was just about what rules and things we needed for the class. When the bell rang I followed Ashley to second period which was one of least favorite classes: Gym. We went to the locker room and I put some nike shorts on and a t shirt and I saw that the other girls have uniforms with the school logo on it and also black pants.Great. I have to buy a uniform.I go out into the gym and sit next to Ashley on the bleachers. There is another boy siting next to her and they are talking so I don't interrupt them."Oh and this is Bailey." Ashley said suddenly. She was looking at me and so was the boy."Oh hi." I said to the boy and gave him a shy smile and which he returned with a smirk. Ah. Egotistical boy. I see how it is so I glare at him."This is my twin brother Preston." Ashley says pointing to the boy next to her."But y'all look nothing alike." I say the first thing that comes to mind. I quickly cover my mouth with my hand over my stupid accusation."It's the okay we are fraternal twins so we don't have to look alike." Ashley said while giggling. Now that I really looked at Preston he has dark brown hair that he keeps styled up and a very attractive face. Catching me staring at him he gives me a wink and goes to the other side of the gym."Don't get under his spell Bailey,he is an asshole to people. Especially girls.""I know I was just trying to find at least one similarity to you from him but I couldn't find anything. Even your personalities are different!" I exclaim. Ashley just chuckles."Nothing I haven't heard before."

:::::

It is finally lunch and Ashley said I could sit with her at lunch. When I get to the cafeteria I see Ashley sitting at a table smack in the middle of the cafeteria. I walk up to it and look at Ashley who was sitting by Jason."Hey Bailey come sit down and I will introduce you to everyone." She says. I sit across from her and I am in between Preston and this other girl who is smacking her gum to loud and is filing her nails."So you already know Preston. The girl filing her nails is Brooke."Brooke has light brown hair and dark brown eyes. She would be really pretty if she didn't have all that makeup on. "The girl next to Brooke is Melissa."Melissa was reading a book when she looked up and I saw that she had really pretty gray eyes and light brown hair."Hi." She said shyly and went back to reading her book."Then that is Graham." She says pointing to the person next to Preston.He looked angry. He had jet black hair and piercing blue eyes. He was muscular and looked tall even though he was sitting down."Okay so this is everybody. So how was your day so far?""Long and boring." Preston said scooting closer to me which causes me to scoot closer to Brooke who looks at me agitated."I wasn't asking you." Ashley said glaring at her brother and Preston just shrugged."My day was okay I mean I didn't get lost so that's a bonus." I said and everybody laughed except Brooke who looked annoyed. Even Graham laughed."So where are you coming from?" Jason asks."I was born in England but when I was two we moved to the United States and just have been moving around from time to time." I say with a shrug."Awe if you would have stayed in England longer you could have gotten an accent." Graham said. I totally misinterpreted he actually doesn't look that angry."I did have an accent till I was four and then I slowly got an American accent."I said."That's so cool so where have you all been?""I have been to California, Tennessee, Flordia, Maine, and even Hawaii.""Wow that's a lot of places to live." Ashley said. I noticed that nobody had school lunches at the table."Yeah. Is the school lunch here good?"I ask curiously."Nope not at all unless you like dog food." Preston said. "Ew." I said. Then the bell rang and I went to my sixth hour class.

:::::

It was finally the end of the day and I got into my car but I saw a note on my car. I got out and got the note from my windshield. I opened it up and it said:

THE HYBRID

I know what you are.

I looked confused just in case the person who left the note was still around. I know how to deal with these situations so I just laugh at it and then crumple the piece of paper.I get in my car and go home which is only a few minutes away from the school.When I walk in my mom is sitting on the couch watching tv."Hey honey how was school?" She asks."Hold up I need to go take my contacts out." I say and go to the bathroom and take my contacts out.I walk back in the living room and plop on the couch."So how was it?""It was fine I met a lot of people. Since apparently the head cheerleader and also head of student council spilt coffee on me this morning.""That sounds great. Besides the coffee on your shirt. So did you meet any supernaturals.""Well the head cheerleader was a mermaid. Her boyfriend, Jason, is a werewolf. There is also a vampire in my first hour class.""Okay but they can't smell you can they?""No remember I can cover my scent of I want to." I say rolling my eyes jokingly."I know. I know I am just looking after my little girl." She said and gives me a hug and a peck on the cheek."So pizza?" She asks.Pizza yum.

~chapter 2~

I woke up, put my contacts in, and got dressed. "Mom I'm leaving now!" I called when I got to the door to leave."Okay have a good day and be safe!" She called before I closed the door and went to my car. When I got to school I saw the tables weren't there anymore and people were standing around talking. I walked around the school trying to find Ashley but I couldn't find her."Looking for someone?" Someone said and I jumped. I looked behind me and it was just Jason."Yeah I was looking for Ashley since she is the only person I know here." I said a little shyly."Come on let's go hang out with the group from yesterday." He said and started walking away and I started walking next to him."So how do you like the school so far?" He suddenly asked."It's fine. The people are much nicer here than they were at my last schools." I said with a shrug. At my last school people would bully me for how skinny I was. I was really skinny but I just couldn't gain any pounds because I had really high metabolism."How were they at your last school?" He asked."Judgmental." I said."There are some people like that at this school but we just ignore them.""That's awesome.""Did you do the math homework last night?" He asked. Me and Jason share math and English together and our teacher gave us this worksheet to see where we stand in the class."I did. Did you?""That's why I'm asking I kinda need to copy yours."I rolled my eyes at him and chuckled."Nope sorry I'm not that type of person ." I say. I see the group and I start walking towards them. Jason is right behind me."Please this one time?" He asks and I turn around and he has his puppy dog eyes on. It's kinda of a coincidence since he is a werewolf. "Fine." His face lit up. "But only this first time. After that your not getting anything from me." I say and start getting the worksheet from my book bag. I handed it to him and went talk to the group."Hey gorgeous." Preston said wrapping his arm around my shoulder. I quickly pushed his arm off to witch he frowned at."O rejected." Said Graham. Preston just gave him the middle finger."Sorry don't like people in my personal space." I say and shrug. Preston looks hurt but then he puts his smirk back on."So you never told us what brought you to this shit hole of a town." Graham said looking at me."Well my mom just wanted a quiet town to settle in and I guess she liked it here." I said. "Now off the topic of me do any of you play sports or anything?" I asked them."I do tennis." Melissa said."Me and Graham do football and baseball." Preston said giving me a smirk."Agh typical egotistical jocks." I joke."Ow." Graham said pointing to his heart. "That hurt. It's true for Preston," that earned him a slap on the shoulder," but not for me." I laughed at them and then looked at Brooke she just rolled her eyes."The only sport she does involves a janitor's closet and a random dude." Jason whispered in my ear. I shuddered a little at that."Why do you hang out with her if she's a whore?" I ask Jason making my voice a whisper."I don't know that is up to Ashley." Jason says. Just then Ashley's joins the group looking really refreshed even though she just had cheerleading practice. Jason wrapped his arm around her shoulder and kissed her on the cheek.

I had that once. I say in my head. I shake that thought out of my head. That was a long time ago.

"How was cheerleading practice?" Jason asked Ashley."Long. Miss Myers was pushing us to our limits even though it is like 7:00 in the morning." She says with a frown."That sucks. Why does she practice y'all so hard?" I ask."We have championships in a few weeks and she wants us to have the routine absolutely perfect." Ashley says."She must pressure you even more since you are the cheerleading captain." I say."I know right she just needs to chill sometimes." Ashley says. The bell rings and Ashley, Jason, and me walk to our first class."No matter how many times I have taken this class I still hate it." I whisper to myself."What do you mean by that?" Ashley asks. I look at her and then smile."I am a little advanced in my studies so I have kinda learned this already but they are making me take it again." I lie."Oh that means you can help me with my homework!" She hugs me and I just chuckle."Don't count on that. I asked her for the math worksheet and she gave it to me but I feel like she won't give it to me again." Jason said."Exactly." I say as we enter the classroom and take our seats."Aww I'm going to keep my free pass for when I really need it." Ashley joked. Just then the teacher walked in and she started the class.

I was asleep when the bell for second period rung. I got out of my seat and headed towards my second period with Ashley. "Why do you let Brooke enter your group she seems kinda mean." I ask her in the locker room for gym. "Well the thing is me, her, and Preston grew up together so we have been friends forever. She wasn't always mean. It's just that ever since Preston rejected her she went cold." Ashley said with a frown."What do you mean Preston rejected her?" I ask."Brooke fell in love with Preston but Preston was waiting for his ma-I mean he didn't like her that way so he rejected her and she just became cold." If Preston was waiting for his mate why does he try to hit on me? Obviously we aren't mates. Are we?"Hello?" Ashley was waving her hand in my face. "I asked you if you were ready but I think you zoned out." She said looking at me curiously."Oh I was just thinking it over. I mean she really went cold after one guy rejected her?""Yeah I don't understand it either." Ashley said and we walked in to the gym."Hey little sis and Bailey." Preston said coming up to us."You're older by two minutes." Ashley said punching Preston on the shoulder."Whatever I am still older.""When is y'all's birthday anyway?""January 1." They said at the same time. They looked at each other a glared and I chuckled."Y'all are definitely siblings anyway so y'all were literally the New Years baby?" "Well I was." Preston said. "I was born exactly at midnight and Ashley was born two minutes after at 12:02.""Yeah we were born prematurely and I had some problems but it's all good now."Ashley says. "We were supposed to be born in March but we were New Year's babies.""That's awesome." I say."Yeah so when is your birthday?" Preston asks."July 20th.""Oh I don't like summer birthdays." Ashley says."Why not?" I say with a fake frown."Because it's always hot down here in Louisiana. Also we don't have school so no one can really wish you happy birthday.""Not if you don't have an iPhone." I said."Oh that reminds me I need your number." Ashley says."Why?" I ask."So we can hang out offer school duh." She says I grab my phone out the pocket of my shorts and unlock and give it to her."Who is this?" She asks and she points to my wallpaper. It was a picture of me and Daniel. "Um I need to change that." I said grabbing my phone and changing my background."Who was he because he is a hunk." Ashley says and Preston scoffs."That was just an ex boyfriend." I said looking at the ground. Good thing the couch started class or else I wouldn't have made it through this class without crying.

::::

I got to 7th period: History. I saw that Ashley wasn't here. She was here today and she does have this class with me. I wonder where she is? I shake my doubt off my shoulder and start trying to pay attention to class.

Key word: trying.

I felt like someone was looking at me. When I was done with the feeling I looked around the room and met the eyes of Mark. Mark was starring at me like he was analyzing me. I felt uncomfortable and just turned back to the front of the class.

I was on my way to my car when I saw Ashley heading towards hers with Preston. I went over there just before they got in the car."Hey Ashley why weren't you in seventh period today?"Ashley froze for a second and then relaxed a bit."I alternate classes every other day so that's why I wasn't in class." She lied. I could tell she was lying by the way her heart sped up and a droplet of sweat went down her forehead. I shrugged it off because it probably had to do with her being a mermaid and all. "Okay well I'll see you tomorrow."I heard here breath out a breath."We need to be more careful about who we are around her." I heard Preston say before he got into the car.I kept walking to my car and drove home.

:::::

When I got home I had a bunch of text messages from Daniel:

Babe

Please answer me

I am soo sorry

I still love you

I just lost control

Please answer me

Why does my brother say that you are were he is?

I shot up from my bed at that last text. I texted him back.

What do you mean? :/

He said that you moved to where he was hiding.

But you don't know where your brother is right?

No but I could ask him and find out where you are.

Please don't I don't want to see you ever again

I'm sorry please forgive me.

I didn't answer him because I was to focused on wondering why Mark would rat me out especially after helping me in the first place. My phone dinged again from another text message but it wasn't from Daniel it was from Ashley:

Do you want to come to my party this weekend?

Yeah it's going to be at your house?

Yeah me and Preston are hosting it.

Sounds good.

We still need to talk about what happened between you and that hunk of a man.

How about tomorrow at school and not around Jason or he might get jealous.

Sounds like a plan. Lol.

I put my phone down and I started my homework that my teacher thought was necessary to give us.

DingDing Ding

I looked at my phone and saw they were from Daniel so I silenced my phone and started doing my homework again.

:::::

" You look absolutely stunning in the dress." Daniel whispered in my ear as we walked in to the club. "Thank you I picked it out especially for you." I said and pulled at his collar and gave him a kiss on the lips. His lips were so soft. His hair which was pitch black which was cut neatly to his ears but his bangs almost went to his eyes. His dazzling green eyes looked at me with some much love and want. "I love you." He said."I love you too." I said to him and we went up to the bar and had some drinks. After about an hour Daniel was drunk and was dancing on the dance floor. Daniel came up behind me and took my hand and lead me to a VIP area in the back. He opened one of the doors and there were beds. He lead me to the bed. I thought we were going to have one of those steamy make out sessions like we always have but Daniel was much rougher this time and he wouldn't stop."Daniel please stop." He didn't listen and took off my dress."Daniel! stop!" I cried."Don't deny that you want me baby." He said. His voice was much huskier and it was sexy but I didn't want to make love when he was drunk and I was pretty close to drunk."Daniel stop." I cried. I was scared beyond belief. I was still a virgin and I didn't want to lose anything tonight. I wasn't ready."No." He said and ripped my panties off. He started pulling down his jeans and I had enough.I looked at him straight in the eyes and compelled him."You are going to stop. You are going to get me some new underwear and then you are going to leave me. Also get back dressed before you doing anything." I said with disgust. I have never seen Daniel this way and it scared me. Since Daniel was a vampire it took a lot for him to get drunk and when he was drunk he got what he wanted. But not this time.

I woke up with sweat dripping down me. That nightmare always scares me. If he wouldn't have stopped, I would have been raped. I didn't want that. I thought Daniel wasn't like that but apparently he was. I don't know what compelled me to keep that wallpaper. Maybe it was because I still loved him. I don't know.

~chapter 3~

M ark's pov

The afternoon after the first day of school.

I still can't believe she is here.

Why did she have to move here out of all places?

Daniel is going to find her and then he is going to find me.

Then he is going to kill me.

Bailey came running into the castle and was in my room packing my bag to leave this damn place. I heard a door slam and I wondered what was wrong. All the walls are soundproof so I couldn't find out what was happening. Then I heard Daniel come in a run up the stairs. "Bailey!" He knocked on her door.

"Bailey open the damn door!" He pounded on her door.

By the silence I am pretty sure that Bailey didn't open the door. I heard Daniel grunt and then heard him stomp off and then leave. I heard Bailey open the door and then she was at my door.

Knock knock

"Come in!" I yelled.

I heard her come in and she sat on my bed. "What happened?" I asked still packing my stuff.

"Where are you going?" She asked avoiding my question.

"Away from here." I said still wondering what could have happened to make the golden couple lose control.

"Why?" She said. She looked sad and she looked like she was about to burst out crying.

"My dad wants me to marry the slut Samantha but I know my mate is out there I just know." I said.

"I wish I could have a mate." She said.

Daniel made sure that she wouldn't. He was the one to turn her into a hybrid. Greedy bastard. Of course she didn't know that.

"Maybe he is out there somewhere." I lied to her. I didn't want her to lose hope in love. Love is always out there even for the most vicious monsters.

"Can I come with you?" She asked. I froze in my place.

"No." I said sternly.

She broke out into tears. Shit I can't deal with this. After some thinking I made my decision.

"Please stop crying," I went over there and kneeled in front of her," I will take you to the airport and get you a ticket so you can back to your mom and then y'all can figure it out from there."

She stopped crying and looked at me and gave me a small smile that looked forced.

"Thank you. I never want to see this place again." She said and got up from off my bed and I stood up and looked at her.

"Me either."

I got home from the first day of school and went to my house. I have a small house with only two bedrooms but it is where I have been for the past 20 years. I have been going to that some high school for 20 years. I make sure to compel the teachers after school ends so they don't ask questions when I come to be a senior again for the next year.

Ring ring

I look at my phone and it is an unknown number. I let it ring a little more and then answer it.

"Hello?" I ask.

"Well isn't it my baby brother. Long time no talk." I froze at that voice. The voice I haven't heard since me and Bailey left that stupid castle.

"Daniel?"

"Who else would it be dumbass?"

"How did you get this number?"

"I have my ways. I also know that Bailey is there with you. I want to know where you are so I can find her."

"No why would I give you my location? I have heard of what you become since Bailey left. You turned off your emotions and you became a heartless monster." I spat in the phone.

"But the thing is... I need Bailey. She is my mate." He said putting the emphasis on 'need.'

"The thing is she is hybrid. A new species. So we don't even know if she would have a mate because you turned her into a vampire before she transformed into her wolf creating a brand new species. That new species has some bad consequences." I said flatly.

"SHE IS MINE! SHE WILL ALWAYS BE MINE!" He yelled into the phone. I hung up and then crushed my phone on to the ground. Don't want him tracking my phone.

I went to go take a shower and observed the little tattoo on my hip. It was a simple flame but I don't remember where I had gotten it from. I think I was born with it but I'm not sure.

Next day at school

I went to school and Ashley came up to me. She didn't really like me and I don't know why. She was a bitch to me so I was mean to her.

"Ashley." I said flatly.

"Hey Mark I was wondering if I can talk to you in private real quick?" She asked a little to nicely.

"Sure." I said and walked around to one of the janitor closet's I gestured for her to come in and lock the door.

"What do you want?" I asked being a little nicer.

"Did we really have to come into the janitor's closet? People are going to think we are doing something in here." She said with concern in her eyes.

"Why do you care? You already cheated on Jason so it doesn't matter." I said bluntly knowing exactly what she wanted to talk about. She glared at me and I smirked."About that do you still have the pictures?" She asked fiddling with her nails that I know she does when she is nervous.

"Yep." I said popping the "p."

She glared at me. "When are you going to get rid of those?!" She yelled at me.

"When you tell him the truth! You need to stop acting like you are perfect when you are not!" I yelled at her and then suddenly realizing how close we are together. I gulped.

"I can't do that! It will break his heart!" She yelled. "It was a drunken mistake and I regret it everyday!"

"Well you need to live up to your mistakes." I said bluntly and then walked out of the closet and storming out of school. No way was I dealing with all of this on my own.

~chapter 4~

Ashley's p.o.v

I hate Mark.

He needs to delete those pictures.

It was one mistake.

One BIG mistake.

Flashback:

I was at a party. I was drunk out of my mind and Jason and me had just gotten into a fight.

It's his fault for going to that stupid werewolf camp all summer were there were other werewolves that were girls and that he could easily trade with me.

I think I am a little paranoid.

How can I not?

He can be fucking some other chick.

Oh my god. He is.

Fine Jason. Let's play.

I grabbed the first boy I saw and kissed him.

Eventually he lead me upstairs but of course someone saw me and took a picture.

Mark.

He took pictures of me kissing the boy and then him leading me upstairs and me going willingly.

That night I lost my virginity to someone I didn't want to lose it too.

Mark is such an ass. Why can't he just keep his stupid mouth shut?

I walked into my first hour class and Bailey and Jason looked at me weirdI sat next to Jason and he immediately leant over and asked"Where were you?"

"Just running a little late." I lied through my teeth

"What's wrong you look upset." He said looking at me in concern.

"Nothing just my mom." I said but it was true. This morning me and mom got into another fight sadly. We never have a normal conversation. This morning she was blaming me for something that Preston did. Like really? It was obvious he did it.

Throughout the day I was just a foul mood but I didn't take it out on anyone like I usually do since I wanted to be good friends with Bailey.

"Are we going to the place today?" Jason whispered in my ear at lunch.

"Yeah."

There is a place in town that all supernaturals go. We live in a town that is a neutral zone which means that no packs live here. It is where most supernaturals that don't want to get found go. I don't know why my family moved here but we have been since I can remember. I don't know why Jason, Mark, and some other werewolves are here but that is none of my business.

And every time that I ask Jason he changes the subject.

I think I have anxiety. I would ask my mom to get me pills but she wouldn't care and just say get over it.

What a great mother I have.

"What's going on in that little mind of yours?" Jason whispered to me. I must have blanked out because the bell had rung and me and Jason were walking to his car.

"We still have classes to go to." I said.

"It's okay you probably have all the homework done for it anyway." Jason said opening the door to his car for me.

"True." I said.

I am a closet nerd and only my teachers and Jason know that. If I want to make it into a good college I have to keep my grades up. If i don't get a scholarship then I don't know what I will do because God knows my mom won't pay a penny for me even though we are practically loaded.

"So where are we going?" I ask.

"It's a surprise." He said and smirked at me. Jason can be shy when he wants to but when Jason is mischievous he always has a smirk on.

"Uh oh this can't be good." I said as we pulled up to a bar.

=======

Boy was I right.

When we walked in the two people I really don't want to see right now.

Mark and Ethan.

Ethan, the guy I cheated with Jason on.

"Can we go somewhere else?" I asked Jason looking up him pleading.

"No they have a nice pool table here." He said and drug me to the pool table.

After a few minutes of them not seeing us Ethan looked my way and smirked and then saw Jason and glared. He started coming over here with Mark in tow. Mark had a smirk on his face knowing what is about to happen. Ethan came up and gave Jason a forced smile and a bro hug.

"Hey man haven't seen you in a while." Ethan said sitting next to me on the couch a little to close for comfort.

Ever since that night every time Ethan is around he tries to hit on me even though Jason is right there.

"How have you been since werewolf camp?" He asked.

I forgot to mention that he is one of Jason's best friends and a werewolf.

Man I really messed up.

"Oh good just trying to get all the juicy details about what happened while I was gone." Jason said and I gulped.

"Yeah like there was this awesome party and I hooked up with this chick too. Took her virginity." He said looking at me but of course Jason was too engrossed in the game.

"Dang what did she look like?" Jason asked and I scoffed.

"Do you really need to know that?" I snapped at him and he put his hands up in surrender.

"Anyway she was a blonde with really blue eyes." Ethan said and then look at me."She kinda looked like you Ashley are you sure you don't have a missing triplet or something?" Ethan asked and I was really tempted to smack him. Mark joined Jason with pool and is trying to hold in his laughter.

"No are you sure it was blonde it could have been a dirty blonde."I said.

"She was a dirty blonde especially in bed." He smirked and looked me up and down and bit his lip. I was furious.

"Okay if all your going to talk about is sex then I am leaving." I said as I left the building and then walking home.

Only to be hit on the head and then drug into a black van before I blacked out.

Awesome.

====

Author's note:

Ashley at the top.

-chapter 5-

Jason's p.o.v.

I watched as Ashley left the bar and I almost went after her before Mark stopped me.

"She's not worth it." He said and I looked at him confused.

"Dude you don't want to show him. It's not worth it." Ethan said getting up from the couch.

"What do you mean? What do you have to show me?" I asked, totally and utterly confused about what they are talking about.

"Fine but if you or her don't tell him then I will show him." Mark said and walked out.

I watched him leave and I looked back at my friend and he looked guilty and then he went to an emotionless face and looked at me.

"What was he talking about?" I asked getting a little angry.

"Nothing." He said and walked out.

What the hell was that supposed to mean?

Obviously he had tell me something and it was something he probably regretted or not. I don't know. And what did Mark mean when he said 'I will show him'? What is going on?

I stopped playing pool and put the cue up and walked out. I was walking home when I felt like someone was watching me.

I turned around to see that no one was there. I shrugged it off and kept walking. I got to my house and saw that my step-dad's car was there.

That's weird he usually isn't home by now.

Oh shit I forgot my car at the bar.

If someone sees it they might get the wrong impression. I told myself that it is okay and then walked into my house.

The first thing I noticed was that my mom didn't greet me.

"Mom?" I called through the house but no one answered.

"Eric?" I called. Eric is my step-dad who my mom married 3 years after my dad died when I was ten. I don't like Eric so I never called him my dad.

I walked into the living room and saw the most disturbing sight.

Eric's hands caressing the breasts of a blonde that definitely wasn't my mom since she was a brunette.

"What the fuck is this?" I growl out. My voice is deeper and I can feel my wolf trying to take control.

"Shit." Eric mutters and gets away from the blonde and I glare daggers at him.

The blonde quickly puts her clothes on and then does the stupidest thing,

"See you at work tomorrow." Winks at Eric and then leaves.

Slut.

"How long?" I ask while still trying to get my wolf under control. Eric knows that me and my mom are werewolves and also knows not to get us ticked off.

"A year." When he said that I saw red and I felt my wolf, Marcus, take over.

Marcus' p.o.v

"What the fuck is your problem?" I ask the piece of shit that I have trapped by the throat on the wall.

"I have been seeing her for a year." He says and he doesn't even seem guilty about it.

"Don't you feel at least a little guilty for what you have done? All these years committed to my mom and it is all washed away because of what?" I demand.

"Your mom and me have been having some problems lately.."

"So you go fuck another chick?" I growl at him. He flinches and that gives me satisfaction.

"Well you see.." He starts.

"What?" I growl.

"Your mom doesn't want you to know this but she filed for divorce about a month ago and we still have to get the papers ready." He says leaning more into the wall like I am going to attack him any minute.

I slowly feel Jason gaining control.

Jason's p.o.v

What?

I slowly let my hands down from Eric's neck and then slump onto the couch.

"When were you going to tell me?" I ask looking up at him. He doesn't even seem bothered by the fact that he is divorcing his wife, my mom.

Oh my gosh. How is my mom getting through this?

"We were going to tell you as soon as the papers were finalized which was going to be in the next week."

"Does she know about all the affairs?"

"No and she doesn't need to." He says glaring at me trying to be intimidating. He might be a few more inches taller than me but he is lanky and barely has any muscle on him.

I glare back at him."Well I should tell her because it doesn't matter now since y'all are getting a divorce."

"YOU ARE NOT GOING TO TELL HER BECAUSE SHE DOESN'T NEED TO KNOW!" He shouts.

"Yes she does she deserves that at least." I say and go to the door."If you don't tell her than I will." I sat turning back and looking at him.

"Please don't. I don't want to break her heart more." He says and looks at the ground finally looking guilty.

"To bad because you have a week before I tell her myself." I say and then walk out the house slamming the door.

======

I was walking towards the bar when I felt the same feeling I had before. Like someone was watching me.

I looked around but no one was there. I shrugged it off and kept going.

Then a felt a needle go into my neck and something injected into me.

Wolfsbane.

"The hell?" I said before I feel to the ground.

"Night Night little wolf." Said a voice before I went into darkness.

====

Author's note

Well as you can see I am updating more often and that is because I FINALLY got my computer to work so I can update faster.

About the whole divorce thing I don't know how it long it actually takes to file for divorce but what I have is probably not accurate so please don't leave comments and be like"OMG that is so wrong why are you so stupid?" like really no one wants to here those kinds of things.

Anyway next week is Thanksgiving.

Wow this year is going by quickly.

Just to think I started this book so many months ago and it feels like forever.

Anyway who do you want to play the people in this story leave suggestions and I probably will mostly likely look at them.

-h

-chapter 6-

M ark^^

Mark's p.o.v

I walked out the bar and then sped to my house using my vampire speed. I got there to see the door kicked open. I opened it up and there lay hundreds of dead bodies.

"What the actual-" I didn't get to finish my sentence because someone walks into the room with blood dripping down his chin.

"Hello brother." He says.

I glare at him and then walk towards him and slam him against the wall.

"What the hell are you doing here Daniel?" I ask but then at vampire speed he has me pinned up on the wall.

"What? I can't visit my favorite brother?" Daniel says getting close to my face and letting me smell his breath.

Blood.

"Ahh I see your still on that little diet of yours?" He says and now I know that my eyes must have been turning red.

I take a deep breath but that only worsens when is smell all the dead bodies with some blood still left in them.

I turn towards brother and say " Get them out of here and I will talk to you." I say and I feel my fangs elongated. He smirks but then lets me down.

"By the way I am your only brother." I say before he starts deposing the bodies. I went into the kitchen because I am going to need a drink if I am going to talk to that lunatic.

==

About an hour later, Daniel had finally disposed of all the bodies. He takes a seat at the table in the kitchen.

"So what do you want talk about?" I ask taking a sip of my fifth beer. I don't feel drunk I need about ten do the trick.

"Bailey." He says simply before getting up and getting a drink for himself and then sitting back down.

"No surprise. But what do you want from her she doesn't want to see you again." I say bluntly. I don't care about how he feels. What he did to Bailey was wrong and disrespectful.

"She does want to see me because I am her mate."

"Bullshit." I say simply. Another reason I don't talk to my brother is because he is a lunatic when it comes to Bailey.

"She is my mate and you know it."He says and I can see him start getting angry.

"Okay then how did she survive all this time without you by her side. They say that if you aren't by your mates side for a long time you get weak. Obviously she is unaffected by the distance that y'all have had. Plus she is a new breed so she doesn't have to have a mate." I say simply.

Daniel looks at me and then slams his drink on the table and then walks out. A few seconds later I hear the door slam and I know that he is gone but I don't know if he will come back.

====

I was in my bed when I heard a noise coming from the kitchen. I ignored thinking it was Daniel. I rolled over and tried to go to sleep.

Key word- tried

A few seconds had passed and I heard slamming and things getting broken. I groaned and then got up.

I walked into the kitchen and saw a figure standing near the sink thinking it was Daniel.

"There is a guest room down the hall to the right across from my room. You can sleep there." I said and then turned around. I started walking down the hallway when I heard chuckling. That didn't sound like Daniel.

"Ahh I was wondering when the dead would rise." The figure said. He had a very deep voice and kinda creepy kind of vibe from him.

"Who the hell are you?" I asked.

"Your worst nightmare." He said before pulling out a bottle throwing the contents on me. The bottle stung and I knew then that it was mirvane.

"What the hell?" I said before dropping to the ground. The man came up and then snapped my neck.

That asshole just tried to kill me.

=====

Author's Note

Hello Hello Hello how are you doing?

Hope you are doing good.

Because I'm not.

I am stuck laying in my bed because I am sick.

So I thought I would update for y'all

I hope get better before next week

Okay I was hoping that with re editing with this story I could get my reads on this story higher than a 100 on each chapter. That is my goal now if i don't reach that goal I am going to ask y'all what I should do to make this story better.Okay that's it.

-h

-chapter 7-

Bailey's p.o.v

Bailey's fangs.....^^^

The day everybody else gets kidnapped.......

I didn't go to school today.

I woke up and I saw that my eyes were glowing and when I put the color contacts in they just glowed right through them.

"Mom!" I shouted.

"Yes Bailey?" She called.

"Can you come here. We have a problem!" I shouted getting a little nervous.

I heard footsteps and then mom came into my room. I looked at her and she looked shocked.

"That's impossible. You haven't even found your mate yet." She said coming towards me. She took my face in her hands and then sniffed in my scent and then she opened her eyes shocked.

"Bailey have you've meet anyone that gives you butterflies or just makes you happy when you are around them?" My mom asked.

"No?" I asked getting really confused.

"Damn then it's not that but something is wrong." She said rubbing her chin. She always did that when she was thinking.

"I can't go to school like this they will now who I am!" I said getting frustrated.

"Don't worry honey you don't need to go to school. You won't even leave this house without my knowledge. Got it?" She said looking sternly me.

"Yes mam." I said and then plopped on my bed.

"Okay well I am going to back outside and work on the garden a bit." She said and then walked out.

I took my phone out and I saw that I had a new message.

Bailey, I am really sorry for what I did. Can you please forgive me? - Daniel

Okay this was the fifth time I had to change my phone number but he always gets it doesn't he?

I put my phone down but then realize that I have to text Ashley to say that I am not going to school today.

Hey Ashley just wanted to let you know that I'm not going to school today. I know how you are so I didn't want you to freak out. Be back tomorrow :) -Bailey

I put my phone down and then laid back in bed wanting to sleep. I laid down and fell asleep.

=====

By the time I woke up it noon and school would be out in like two hours. I went to the kitchen and looked around for my mom but she wasn't there. I went back to the kitchen to see a note taped to the refrigerator.

Went shopping. Be back in few hours. - Love Mom

Okay so I was left alone for a few hours. I went to the bathroom and checked my eyes to see that they were still glowing. Sighing I went into the kitchen and opened the fridge to get a blood bag and see if that would help. I grabbed it and then went to the mirror and looked at my eyes while drinking.

Nothing happened.

I took the blood bag and threw it away. Deciding to do something constructive I started cleaning up.

Two hours later of doing that I heard that front door slam open.

"Mom? Is that you?" I say walking into the living room to see the man standing there.

Definitely not my mom.

"Who the hell are you?" I ask starting to get nervous but I can easily take this guy.

"I'm just here to get what my boss wanted."He said before coming towards me.

I backed away and then he tries to grab me but I kick him where the sun doesn't shine.

"Bitch." He said before grabbing my leg and dragging me across the floor to the front door.

"Wouldn't it look weird if they saw you dragging me out of my house?" I said. With that he put a rag on my mouth. I started to feel dizzy.

"That's why I am going to carry you bridal style so people think you are asleep." He said.

"Where are you taking me?" my mind slowly starting to shut down.

"To the boss." He said before putting me in the backseat of his truck and me blacking out.

====

I woke up being in a dark cell.

Great. I slowly started opening my eyes but I couldn't move my body. I felt a stinging pain on my wrists and I knew that they must be cuffed. I looked around a saw someone sitting in the cell across from me.

"Finally you wake up." He says. Wait I know that voice.

"Jason?' I asked. I saw him nod and know I am just totally confused.

"What are we doing here?" I asked trying to sit up but my body is still weak from whatever that man gave me and then these stupid handcuffs.

"I don't know but I think I broke a nail." Said another voice and I knew then that it was Ashley.

"Wow Ashley way to think of yourself in this situation." Jason says sarcastically.

"Sorry I still need to work on that." She said apologetically.

"It's okay. It's better then what it was before we dated." Jason said.

"Yeah I was a complete bitch." Ashley said and I can hear the sorrow in her voice.

Just then I heard someone coming down the stairs.

"Shhh be quiet someone is coming down the stairs." Jason said and then backed away into the corner of the cell. I could feel my body again so I did the same and I can hear Ashley do the same.

"How could you hear that?" I asked trying to sound human.

Shit my eyes. I don't have my color contacts in. I just hoped they stopped glowing.

Just then the door opened and two men were dragging someone into a cell.

Death. That's what I smelt. It was a vampire. I went towards to the cell bars and tried to peak through only to get stung. I knew that the bars where laced with wolfsbane and mirvane. I still tried to look and what I could see was the tattoo he had on his hip. I gasped because I know that tattoo anywhere.

It was Mark.

Then someone else came into the room and then the other two men stepped out.

"Ahh I see that most of you are awake." The man said. The man was tall and had power radiating off of him. But something was off about him. He had this slight evil vibe about him.

"Rogue." Jason growled.

"Ahh yes little pup." He said. Then the man looked at me and started walking towards my cell and I backed away scared. His eyes were completely black. I knew then that he was a rogue werewolf.

Rogue werewolves lose themselves to their wolves. The only way you become rogue is if you get banned from the pack and don't go into neutral ground. The rogues that choose to stay in pack boundaries become crazy with pack lost and disconnection thus losing their mind and their wolf takes over.

"Leave her alone! She is only human!" Jason yells coming towards the cell bars.

"Jason don't touch the bars!" I yell but he is too late and he howls in pain.

"Oh my gosh Jason are you okay?" Ashley yells but she can't touch the bars either because of the fairy dust. Fairies are extinct because the rogues exterminated and used them for the fairy dust to make cells for mermaids. Mermaids are allergic to fairy dust like vampires are allergic to mirvane and werewolves are allergic to wolfsbane.

"Ahh so I see what is going on." the man says looking at me and smirking.

"I don't know what you are talking about." I said getting a little nervous because of the secret he is about to probably reveal.

"You kids don't know that Bailey is a-" He gets caught off by a loud roar and we look towards Mark's cage where he looks pissed.

"Where the fuck am I?" He roars. I back away because he is emitting his royal power. It is strong maybe even stronger than the mine.

The man smirks." I see I have myself a royal. This is great. I thought you were a regular vampire but by judging by the red eyes you are royal. Which one are you Mark or Daniel?" I flinch at Daniel's name.

"I don't have to answer your question." Mark says calming down a bit.

"Okay but back to what I was saying before. I am guessing you don't know what Bailey is." The man says before turning back to me and smirking.

"What is he talking about Bailey?" Jason says. He looks at me concern and I gave him a wary smile. Just then I drop my scent that I have been hiding from Jason and Ashley.

Jason sniffs the air and then his eyes turn black.

"MATE!" He calls out and then tries to break the bars but he backs up when he stings himself.

"What?" Ashley, Mark, and I say at the same time.

The man starts chuckling but it isn't light it is an evil chuckle.

"Well this just got more interesting." He says and then moves towards Ashley's cage.

"Well I guess your boyfriend just found his mate." He said and then unlocked the cage and dragged her out by the hair. Ashley screams in pain thrashing around trying to get out of his grip.

I heard Jason growl. "Just because Bailey is my mate doesn't mean I don't care about Ashley." He says and he looks at the man darkly.

Just then then man made Ashley go to Mark's cage.

"Lift up your shirt." The man order's Ashley.

"Hell no." She says trying to get out of his grasp that he now has on one of her arms.

"Just so we can see the tattoo on your hip." He says.

" No because you don't need to see it." She says while crossing her arms knowing that she isn't going to get out of his death grip.

"But he does." The man says tipping his head towards Mark.

"Why would I need to see it?" Mark asks looking at the man like he was crazy.

"Look whatever your name is. I am not lifting my shirt." Ashley says and glares at him.

"My name is Xavier."

"I don't give a shit what your name is. Let me go." Just then Xavier took Ashley and put her in front of himself and then lifted her shirt on the left side.

There was a tattoo just like Mark's hip.

They are mates.

"Mate?" Mark says.

Ashley looks at him and I mean REALLY looks at him. Then her eyes widen in shock.

"NO NO NO! I can't be mated to him!" She says trying to get away from Xavier.

"Aww too bad sweetheart y'all are mates." He says and then drags her back to her cell.

"I am going now so y'all can sort out your problems." He says and then walks out.

"Wow this is one fucked up situation." Mark says.

I nod my head in agreement.

-chapter 8-

Jason^^^^

Bailey's p.o.v

"Bailey?" Jason asked getting my attention.

"Yes?" I said a little nervous.

"What are you?" Jason says and then looks into my eyes but then he gasps.

"Your eyes are red." He says and then tries to look closer but he has to back away from the bars.

"Yeah I know." I say looking down ashamed.

"So all this time you knew who we were?" I nodded and then he looked angry.

"Did you know that we were mates?" He asks angry.

"No." I say truthfully. I don't know why I didn't know but I just didn't.

"So what are you exactly?" Ashley asks.

"I'm a-" Just the the door opened a four guys walked and by their eyes I know they are rogues.

"Boss wants to see all you now." One of them say before they opened my cage and put the cloth on my face.

"Not this again."I say as I pass out and I hear a growl.

=====

I woke up to being in a chair in a room with my hands tied up.

Awesome.

I looked around and I saw Jason in one corner, Ashley in another, and then Mark.

We were in a room that was all white and we were in metal chairs.

I heard groaning and I looked to see that the rest were walking up.

"God I hate this." Mark says.

"Me too." the rest of us say.

"Ahh looks like y'all are awake." A voice says but it was only us in the room. Then I look up and see a speaker and a camera.

"Hey asshole can you let us out of here?"Jason yells. The man chuckles.

"Nahh I want to do some experiments." Just then the door that blends into the wall opens. Four men walk in and I recognize one of them as Xavier. He smirks and then comes stand by me and the other three stand by the rest of us.

"What kind of experiments?" Ashley asks scooting away from the man next to her and he smirks and winks at her. Which earns a glare from Jason and growl from Mark.

"Touch her and your dead." Mark says and I can see his eyes turning red. I am guessing the mate bond is starting to take action. The man just smirks.

"Okay enough." The man from the speakers say.

"What do you want?" I shout. I was beyond pissed.

"I want to make another hybrid." He says almost like he is sure this is going to work.

"What do you mean another hybrid?" Ashley asks. Mark looks the other way and so do I. I feel the glare of a certain someone looking at me.

"He's talking about you? Isn't he?" Jason asks. I look at him and he generally looks concerned and hurt?

I nod slowly. He looks at me with hurt in his eyes and then looks away shaking his head.

"That's so cool!" Ashley says. She then looks at me and I can see the excitement in her eyes.

I would have laughed but we kinda aren't in the right situation.

"What kind of hybrid are you?" Ashley asks sounding a little too excited for my liking.

"Werewolf and vampire." I say.

"Okay cut the chit chat. Let's get into making another hybrid." the voice says sounding annoyed.

"Whatever why don't you come in here and face us yourself?" I shout at him.

"I will once I know that I can make a hybrid." He says. "Boys take Mark and Jason and put them both in the middle."

The two guys took the chains and then chained them to the ground in the middle of the room.

"Now Mark I need you to turn Jason." The voice says.

"No way." Mark says backing away from Jason.

"You are going to do it or else I will kill your little mermaid." He says and I saw that the guy now has a knife against Ashley's throat.

I heard growl from both Jason and Mark.

"Touch a hair on her head and I will kill you all with my bare hands." Mark said.

"And I'll help." Jason growled at the man.

"Shut up and turn him!" The voice shouted through the speakers.

"No!" They both shouted. Then in a flash both the rogues holding Jason and Mark had a gun pointed to there heads.

NO! MATE MUST NOT DIE!

A was surprised by the new voice. Then I heard pops and cracks and I realized it was coming from me.

"Oh shit." The man said from beside me.

"Oh shit in deed." Said somebody and everybody was looking at me.

Did I say that?

No I did.

Who are you?

Your wolf , Talia.

Oh cool.

Talia's p.o.v

After that I blocked Bailey out. I am different from different wolves. I am bigger and I have a streak of red in my black coat. I also let out a strong wave of power that will make any wolf bow down to me.

"Now I suggest you take those guns and point them to your own heads." I commanded and the two guys did. I then turned to the guy that was next to me.

"I suggest you get the hell out of here before I kill you." The man looked at me and fear and I gave him a wolfy smirk.

He ran out there with his tail tucked between his legs.

"Now you two I suggest that you take those guns and kill yourself."

With one really loud bang they were both dead. I then turned to the last guy which was Xavier.

"Don't miss with me wolfie. I will kill you." Xavier said confidently.

"I think the only one who is about to die is you." I say. Xavier growls and then turns into his wolf. He is smaller than me and I can bet that he used to be a alpha.

"Come on alpha show me what you got." I said and he lunged at me but I ducked and then grabbed on to his neck and ripped it killing him in mid air. He fell to the ground with a bang.

"Nice job well done." Said the voice from the speakers.

"Come in here you coward and show me what you got. You will probably get lucky and get killed instantly and not tortured but that is highly unlikely." I say.

Just then the door opened and a man who was tall and muscular walked in. He had black eyes like the other rogues and had brown hair. He looked older and had a lot of power radiating off of him but not as much as mine.

I growled t him and starting walking towards him but Jason stepped in front of me.

"Dad?" Jason said looking at the man with shock.

"Hello son nice to see you again." He said with a smirk.

=====

Author's note

I am updating as much as I can because next week I might not be able to update at all because I am going to another state for thanks giving.

-h

-chapter 9-

Jason's p.o.v

"What the hell?" I asked poking my dad in the chest.

He just looked at me because we were the same height.

"That's what I get after all this years?" He asked with smirk.

I backed away from him because I couldn't stand looking at him. He isn't the same. He looks the same but instead of the protection that I felt around around. I felt repulsed. His eyes aren't the green that I wished I had inherited but didn't. They were black.

"I thought you were dead!" I said and then punched the wall and I felt my wolf coming back but I still had my cuffs.

The fuck is happening?

"That's what your mom told you?" He asked laughing."Dang she really wanted to spare your feelings and the image of herself."

"What do you mean?" I asked totally confused.

"Your mom cheated on me. She found her real mate and didn't even till me so she had an affair with him. And let's just say that I came home one day and found her mating with him in OUR bed." He said with a grimace.

"What did you do?" I asked because I never heard of him.

"I killed him." He said.

"But I thought you told me that y'all were mates?" I asked confused.

"We weren't. We told you that because we didn't want to tell you the truth." He said.

While I was processing this information I saw that the guys behind my dad had disappeared and then I heard a whimper. I turned around and saw Bailey fall to the ground and she turned back to human. The two guys both syringes and one was empty.

"What the fuck is your problem?" I growled and then launched at them but they plunged the syringe into me and I passed out.

=====

I woke up in the cell that I had early but something was different. I looked around and Bailey wasn't there. They took the cuffs off so I can slowly feel my wolf coming back. I used my wolf hearing and tried to figure out where Bailey was.

Then I heard it....

"I am going to help you get out of here" a voice said and then I heard her voice.

"Daniel, you have to help your brother and my friends to. You can't just rescue me." She said.

"But I don't give fuck about my brother he is an ass and I could care less about your friends." I heard her growl and I knew her wolf must have done that.

"If you aren't going to help them then you can leave without me." She said.

"No Bailey. Fine. Only because I love you. Okay?"

"Whatever just get me out these chains."

Wait what?

Was Daniel her boyfriend?

Who's Daniel brother?

"Mark!" I yelled in my cell.

"What?" he yelled irritated.

"Who's Daniel?" I asked.

"My asshole of a brother." He mumbled.

"Why is he here?" I ask. getting angry.

"Probably to save Bailey." He said slightly annoyed. "and how did you know he was here?"

"I was using my wolf hearing and I heard voice talking to her and she said his name was Daniel and that he should save the rest of us and not just her."

"That little shit was going to leave me ,his own brother, to die." He said and I can hear the angry tone in his voice.

"Well yeah will Bailey convinced to help us too."

"Ahh just like old times." He said with an amusement tone.

"What do you mean by old times?" I ask totally confused. I mean they must have had a past since Daniel did say that he loved her. But she is mine.

"That's not my story to tell." Mark said and then we heard and the door opened and I can smell Bailey and another which smelt like death.

"Great another vampire." Ashley groaned.

"Nice to meet you too." The vampire which I am guessing is Daniel said sarcastically.

Just then Daniel had the key to my cell and opened the cell door. He stepped away and then went to undo Mark's ad Ashley's.

I stepped out of the cell and then went hug Bailey and I felt shocks when she hugged me back.

Then we heard a growl and we looked behind us and we saw Daniel standing there looking pissed with red eyes.

Bailey walked over to him and rubbed his chest and I let out a growl. She looked at me and then did something I didn't know she could do.

Just wait until I get rid of him.

She said in my mind and she turned around and hugged Daniel. I saw him relax and hug her back.

"We are in some deep shit." Mark said walking to the door only to be blocked by some angry looking rogues.

"Great it just got better." Ashley said sarcastically.

"Who let you out?" They growled and then they grabbed Mark and then something unexpected happened the rogue burst into flames.

I looked at Bailey but she shrugged. I looked at Ashley and her eyes were glowing red and she was looking at the rogue angrily.

"DO NOT TOUCH HIM AGAIN" she yelled. It was scary as fuck because her voice made the walls quiver. The other rogue just smirked and put a finger on Mark but he quickly went up into flames too. The next thing I see there are ashes on the ground were the rogues were supposed to be.

"Let's get out of here before we find anything else out." Bailey said exasperated and started heading towards the door but she stopped when we heard Ashley hit the floor.

"Great I got her." Mark said walking over to her and picking her up bridal style. I watched him almost drop her when I knew he probably felt the sparks.

"I'll lead the way so just follow me." Daniel said talking Bailey hand and dragging her out which earned a growl from me but she looked at me with pleading eyes and I covered it with a cough.

After going through some hallways, we strangely didn't run into rogues.

"Where are all the guards?" Mark asked still carrying Ashley.

"Let's just say I was really pissed off when I found out that rogues captured Bailey." Daniel said smirking.

We got to a door and Daniel opened it and it lead to a bedroom.

"Okay behind that bookshelf there should be a tunnel that will lead to my car." Daniel said starting to mess with the books when he pulled on the final one the book shelf opened and it lead to a tunnel.

"Okay I have a little car so it isn't going to fit all of us." Daniel said.

"Me and Bailey can run as our wolves." Daniel turned to me and glared and I glared back.

"Yeah me and Jason can just run as wolves." Bailey said hugging Daniel and he relaxed and hugged her back and mumbled an okay.

We went into the tunnel and when we got out we were in Walmart parking lot.

Daniel's car is right over there. The woods was right behind the Walmart so me and Bailey went over there alone which earned a glare from Daniel.

We shifted into our wolves and we ran to the side of the road away from other people's eyes and searched for Daniel's car. When Daniel's car passed us we started running beside it keeping up with it.

We were finally free.

Until

I will find you my son and you will join me.

-chapter 10-

Ashley's p.o.v

I woke up in a bed that I don't know.

I did the only thing reasonable.

I screamed.

In a second Mark was by my side holding my mouth shut. I gasped because of the sparks I was feeling.

"Are you done?" He asked and I nodded my head.

"Where are we?" I asked looking around. I was in a bedroom that I didn't know. I was in a big kind size bed that I didn't know. The only thing I did know was that Mark was right beside me.

"You are in my room and in my bed." Mark said bluntly sitting in the chair by the bed.

I looked at him and he had dark circles under his eyes.

"How long was I out?" I asked laying back down on the bed.

"A few hours."

"How did we get back the last thing I remember is being locked in a cell with you across from me."

"Well my brother Daniel rescued us from the cell. And let's just say when one of the rogues tried to attack me, you kinda set him on fire." Mark said looking at me expectantly.

"What?! But I am a mermaid and I can only control water!" I said getting nervous.

"I know. I know."

"What is happening to me?" I asked taking his hand and looking in his eyes. He looked at me and he was frowning.

"I honestly don't know." Mark said shaking his head and then running his free hand through his hair. It was then that I noticed that I was still holding his hand. I quickly took my hand away.

"Well I am going to go because I need to uh yeah." With that he left.

I fell back on to the bed.

How could I control fire? I am a freakin mermaid! Plus what creature could control fire? Not any that I know.

I have to ask my mom about this.

Bailey's p.o.v

Me and Daniel got back to my house after dropping Jason off at his house. I walked in and was immediately engulfed into a hug.

"Where the hell have you've been?I have been worrying sick. I thought someone took you!I even called Matilda to help-"

"What you called Matilda?" I asked shocked.

Matilda is a witch that can't be trusted. We were friends with her until she tried to take my powers for herself.

"Uh yes?" My mom looking sheepish.

"WHAT THE HELL MOM SHE ALMOST KILLED ME!" I yelled and she backed away in fear. I went up to her and hugged her feeling bad.

"Sorry just a little worked up because I really don't want to go through that experience again." I said. I pulled away and then mom finally looked at Daniel who was standing awkwardly by the door.

"What the hell is this piece of shit doing her?" My mom growled at Daniel.

"I am the one who saved Bailey and her friends from the rogues." He said not getting intimidated by my mom.

"Rogues?" My mom asked me looking over me looking for any injuries.

"Yeah I will tell you later but I need to speak to Daniel in private. And I mean you don't snoop with your little ears." I said pointing a finger at my mom while grabbing Daniel's hand and leading him to the back door.

Before I closed the door she yelled "My ears aren't small!" Before the door slammed.

I went to sit at the table and gestured to Daniel to sit across from me.

After a few minutes I spoke, "What are you doing here anyway? I made sure to avoid anywhere to where you can find me." I said glaring at him.

"Well I didn't know you were her until I found where Mark was hiding and then I saw you go into the same school as him." He said.

"Why don't you realize that I ran away from you for a reason? You tried to rape me! I wasn't ready yet you don't give a shit about anything except for yourself and what you want." I spit out at him and he looked at me angrily.

"I was drunk! I didn't know what I was doing!" He said looking at me and then slumping in his seat.

He looked me and then said something that caused butterflies in my stomach,"I will always love you. You are incredibly gorgeous. You are shy when you first meet people but when you are more comfortable you have this sarcastic side and is incredibly funny. You have this spark in this eyes that shows that you will not give up until you show that your right in an arguement. When you are around me my heart speeds up and I get really nervous like I am going to say something wrong. I love you so much. It hurts. And I know you are some type of new creature so you might have a mate and you might not but even if you do I will fight to the death for you. I love you so much." By then he was in tears and it looked like something clicked inside of him.

"I am so sorry for what I did to you. I am also sorry for what I did to the people I hurt after you left. I slept with so many women." I cringed at that," I killed them after I was satisfied and then I would go drink random people's blood and then kill them. I didn't care because I was just trying to numb the pain I felt when I lost you." He said and I knew then that I was still in love with him. Even though he messed up, I still love him. I also know that this person sitting across from me with his head in his hands and crying like a baby is so broken and I feel bad because I was part of it.

I got up and I walked up to him. I kneeled in front of him and then put my hands on his cheeks and kissed with all the feelings that I had for him.

"I am so sorry Bailey." He said when we pulled apart.

"I forgive you." I said and then kissed him again.

"I love you Bailey." He said looking at me with some much love and sincerity.

"I love you too." I said meaning every word of it.

===

Author's note

Well then what's going to happen with Jason?

Keep reading and kind out.

And if you don't like this new version of the story please tell me.

Each chapter I try to make it more then a thousand words.

If you want longer chapter's just tell me.

Plus if they are longer then they will most likely be in other p.o.v like in this chapter was two point of views.

-h

-chapter 11-

Jason's p.o.v

I got home and I walked into my mom talking to someone on the phone but once she saw me she hung it up and came running to me

I was quickly engulfed into a bear hug that had me gasping for air when she released me.

"Where have you've been? I have been worried sick!" She says standing there with her hands on her hips and a glare directed towards me.

"I was kidnapped by rogues." I say bluntly remembering what my dad had told me.

She lied to me my whole life.

"Did they hurt you?" She asked scanning my body for bruises.

"No but I did see someone I thought I'd never see." I say looking at her and I saw the fear flash through her eyes.

"You found out didn't you?" She asked and I nodded she walked out and I followed her to the living room. She sat down and patted the seat next to her which I sat in.

"I did love your father but I knew we weren't mates and our fathers forced us to get married and so we did. When I found my mate I was conflicted. The day your father walked in on us I was going to tell him about my mate. I didn't want to get that far but I was pulled by the mate bond. I didn't want your father to find out about it like that. But what he did was someone I had not grown to love,"My mom had tears in her eyes and she looked at me with sadness," He tore my mate off me and then killed him before my own eyes and then he didn't even look sorry. He looked at me and then ran off and so I told you he was dead because that was better than what had happened." She finished and she was broken out in tears and I hugged her.

"I'm so sorry you had to go through with that. I can never imagine that pain you had to go through. But how did you move on from your mate so fast with Eric?" I asked curious to know.

" I knew you needed a father figure in your life and I thought Eric was fit for that."

"Obviously a bad choice." I say and she chuckled.

"So what happened while you were there?" She asked.

"I found my mate-" I started and all of a sudden she was up and squealing like a little girl giving me a big bear hug.

"Can't-breathe." I said between breathes and she quickly looked down at the floor in shame and mumbled an apology.

"Anyway," I say while sitting back down on the couch and my mom did also," I think she has feelings for someone else. Like deep feelings." I say running my fingers through my hair in frustration.

"Oh honey no one can resist the pull of the mate bond and she will come to you." My mom said reassuring. "Now tell me some stuff about her."

"Her name is Bailey. She has really long curly hair that frames her face so perfectly and her eyes are so pretty. The ignite a fire in me that I didn't know. She is shy at first but then she is so funny and sarcastic and just can make anyone love her."

My mom lowly whistles. "Wow son I think you are already whipped." She said while chuckling.

"I know and that's what scares me."

Ashley's p.o.v

I walked into the door of my house to see my parents sitting at the couch crying.

I walk into the room and looked at them a little scared of what happened.

My mom looked up and saw me and she looked so sad.

"Ashley there is something that we have to tell you." My mom said sitting up and then wiping her eyes and fixing her skirt and blouse.

"What?" I asked getting annoyed because they didn't even ask me if I was okay especially since I was gone for few days.

I wonder if I ran away that they would even notice.

"Preston got into an accident and the doctors say he might not make it." She said and then starting to cry again.

"What?" I ask feeling my knees give out on me. I slump down on the floor and start crying. I don't know how long I was there before my mom came up and stood me up.

"Ashley you need to get it together because we are going to the hospital to visit and we don't want you to look awful." She said bluntly and then sniffed the air," please go take a shower you stink." She said and pushed me in the direction of the bathroom. I went into the bathroom and looked at myself in the mirror. Wow I look awful. My mom was right I do stink final smelling the awful stench coming off of me. About 20 minutes later I was dress and headed into the living room. I saw that no one was there and I went into the kitchen but no one was there. I looked on the refrigerator and saw a note.

You were taking to long so we decided to go without you but no worry you will get to see him tomorrow.

-mom

Wow. That made me feel great about myself. They actually left me here? She is the one who told me to go take a shower. Am I really that bad of a daughter?

What did I do to deserve this?

You should have taken a shorter shower.

You shouldn't haven't went to Mark's.

You should have been more careful walking by your self.

Why am I so stupid?

Gosh what if Preston got in a wreck looking for me?

This is all my fault.

I walked to the bathroom and opened a draw and then took out the secret bottom and looked at the blades.

I haven't done this in a while.

But it's my fault.

I should try to make myself worthy of my parents approval.

It's my fault that Preston is in the hospital and could die.

I crumpled to the ground after slitting my wrists five times on each wrist.

I should just run away.

But where?

I thought for a while and then I had an idea and I went to my room and packed a bag.

After that I walked out the front door and walked to the person's house.

I knocked and he opened up wearing only a pair of boxers.

===

-chapter 12-

Mark's p.o.v

After dropping Ashley off at her house I went back to my house and saw Daniel's car and I wondered what he was doing here.

I walked in and saw he was cooking in the kitchen.

That's weird I never seen him cook before.

I walked over to him and he had a big smile on his face.

I looked over at the table and there were three more table mats organized.

'What is going on?" I said looking around and then pinching my self thinking it was a dream.

"Oh I invited Bailey and our parents to dinner." he said and then turned off the stove and put the food on all the plates.

"WHAT?" I roared. There was a reason I ran away. My parents only think about power and they never accept anything beside what they think is right.

Flashback

"Master Mark your father wants to see you." My butler Oliver told me.

I was laying on my bed at the castle and I was reading a book trying to get away from my parents. Which obviously I can't do.

"Thank you Martin." I said and then got up and headed to my father's office.

I knocked and then entered. I saw my parents by my father's desk and then two women and a man sitting on the chairs and couch in the room. I sat on the couch next to one of the women who looked me up and down and gave me a "seductive" smirk and pulling her shirt down a little trying to show her cleavage.

Slut. I scoffed.

"Son that is Samantha. She is the daughter of one of the most powerful vampire covens under us."

"Hi nice to meet you." I said kindly looking at her.

"The pleasure is all mine." She said trying to sound sexy.

Key word is trying. She sounded like a dying cat. Her voice was really squeaky. She was beautiful but her personality just ruined it.

She had long black hair that went down to her waist. She was skinny but curvy at the same time but she wore lot of makeup that probably ruined her complexion and natural beauty. She wore a skirt that left no imagination and shirt that showed way to much cleavage. I scoffed at her and then turned my attention to my dad.

"Why are they here?" I asked leaning back on the couch and scooting away from Samantha as she tried to scoot closer to me.

"I want you to marry his daughter." I choked on my own spit at that and looked at Samantha who looked like she got a great Christmas present and then looked at my dad who had a blank expression on his face.

"Fuck No!" I yelled out after my coughing fit.

"You haven't found your mate yet and that means you need someone to help you lead if I give you throne." my father says while glaring at me.

"I am not marrying that slut!" I yelled and got up off the couch while my father looked pissed and Samantha's mom and dad gasped.

"You shall not talk about people that way!" My father roared standing up behind his desk.

"I can talk however I want." I said bluntly and then walked out determined to get the hell out of this place.

Flashback Over.

"I invited them so we can discuss some things." He said and then the door bell rang. I felt the power radiating through the door and I knew it was my mother and father. I walked there slowly not wanting to deal with this.

I opened the door and my parents were there and they haven't changed. That was obvious since they are vampires.

My dad was still a little taller than me and had amazing posture that just screams"bow down to me". The black hair that I had inherited from him was slicked back but you can see some grays in it. He was wearing one of his many business suits and had is dark blue eyes (that I didn't inherit but Daniel did) glaring at me.

"Hello son long time no see." He said bitterly. My mom slapped him on his arm and glared at him.

"Be nice. You haven't seen your son in many years yet here you are being an asshole to him."

While my dad was ice cold my mom was the complete opposite. She had light blonde hair that definitely contrast my dad's black hair but she makes up in her height at a staggering 5'11. She was tall for a woman. She has light brown eyes that I inherited and she has the warmest smiles.

She quickly wrapped me in a hug.

"I have missed you so much son," and then she slapped me on the back of my head,"don't you ever run away without saying goodbye again." She said, glaring playfully.

I chuckled,"I wouldn't count it as running away if I told you I was leaving." She smiled at me and I knew then how much I have missed my mom.

"Come on in dinner is on the table and Bailey should be here in a few minutes." I said and my dad gave a swift nod and then headed into the house followed by my mom.

Unlike me and Daniel, my parents don't know that Bailey is a hybrid. I think they would be intimidated by the power that she holds and might do some bad things to her. Probably experiment and then try to make more hybrids for their own personal armies. I definitely have to keep the secret from my mom because she doesn't like being intimidated. Just because she is sweet and welcoming she is a beast when she feels threatened and will kill anything that threatens her. That is why she is one of the most feared vampires in the world among my dad, me, and my brother.

"Son this looks great." I hear my mom say as I walk into the dining room. She is sitting at the table with a glass of blood that looks like wine in front of her. My dad is at the end of the table glaring at the food.

"When should Bailey be here?" my father asked suddenly. Then the door bell rings and Daniel goes gets it with a smile.

"Mark how have you've been?" My mom asks looking at me thoughtfully.

"I have been fine. I have been going to school and-" I was cut off by my father's dark chuckle. He looked at me.

"School? Really? That's all you have been doing since you have left? You could have had the throne by now but no you want to go to school?" My father spits out.

"Eric please calm down it is his choice if he doesn't want to take the throne." My mom says glaring at my dad.

"No! Because he could have been married to one of the most powerful covens daughter and leading the vampire world but noooo. You actually went to school and live that boring life." My father scoffs.

"Hey everybody." Bailey says coming in but my father is still glaring at me.

"Oh honey!" My mom says getting up and hugging her. " I have missed you so much!" She backs up and then takes Bailey's face in her hands and glares.

"Why the hell are your eyes red?" My mother spits.

My dad's glare takes off me and then looks at Bailey. Daniel, Bailey, and I freeze.

Oh shit.

-chapter 13-

Dedicated to- @MarrisaParker4 for voting and commenting on my story. :)

Jason's p.o.v

To have Ashley show up at my door was a complete shock.

To have her show up in the middle of the night while I was in my boxers about to go to sleep is another shock.

"Hey?" I ask timidly.

"Hi can I stay here for awhile?" She asks looking around and gives me a small smile.

"Why?" I ask furrowing my eyebrows.

"If you let me stay I will tell you everything." She says and I move so she can get in and then I lead her to the guest room.

When we get in there she flops down on one side of the bed and then I flop down on the other.

"What d-" Before I can speak she covers my mouth with her hand.

"What I am going to tell you is something I never had told anyone but Preston. You might get mad but you need to have an open mind." She says looking at me almost guilty.

I nod my head.

"I have really bad anxiety. Ever since I was little I have had it and my mom refuses to get me the pills for it and sometimes I lose control over it. Sometimes I go into anxiety attacks but it had been years since I have one. The only recent one I have had was about two months ago. Now when I tell you this. You have every reason to be mad and upset but just blame me don't blame the other person." She says and I start getting scared of what she was going to say but I nod anyway.

"It was when you left for werewolf camp and a person at our school had a party. I was drunk. Soo drunk. I was having my thoughts clouded about you at werewolf camp. You with other she-wolves that were better than me and that could provide you with what I couldn't. So I took the first guy and I kissed him," I sucked in a breath at that," I lost my virginity to him and when I woke up that next morning, I ran. When I got to my house I had an anxiety attack. I was scared about what you would think and how my parents would think. I am an awful person and I am so sorry." She said and then started crying. I didn't know what to do.

"Who was he?" I bitterly feeling my wolf come to the surface.

"No one with importance." She said a little to quickly. I sat up then and looked at her.

"Was it someone I know?" I asked and she didn't answer and then my mind flashed to the bar right before we got kidnapped.

"It was Ethan wasn't it?" I spit out and she flinched but she didn't deny it.

I got up off the bed and started pacing the room and running my hand through my hair.

"Jason I don't know what to say or to do but I want to say I'm sorry for putting you through this." She says and then takes her bags and then walks out. I don' know where she is going but I know one thing.

How could my life be so fucked up?

Ashley's p.o.v

I didn't tell him the whole truth just part of it.

I didn't tell him about my mom or Preston or about how my mom would beat me.

When I was little Preston was always put first before me. He would always get the best gifts and my parents loved him. On Christmas Preston would get a big Santa Claus present and many more from my parents and I would get a little small doll and that's it. Preston was always the one my parents paid attention to. When I was about eleven I accidentally cut my wrist while chopping vegetables for my mom and my mom slapped me for getting blood on the vegetables. I also discovered that cuts made me feel better. They made me feel free that I could have more physical pain than emotional. So I started cutting. I would wear hoodies to hide the scars. I was also gaining a lot of weight so my mom forced me into cheer leading. That was the only good thing my mom did but every time I would mess up my routine on the field, I would come home to my mom screaming at me saying that I need to be more attentive. Then if I tell her that it won't happen again she would slap me and say don't talk back to me. I never liked my mom. I still love her because she is my mom but she is a despicable person. Now that I am older she wants me to dress appropriately because if I wear shorts that goes down to my knees I am considered a slut in her eyes. The night I lost my virginity my mom smelt that I was unpure and slapped me across the face and then took a knife and spelt "unpure" on my back. It still leaves the scar today on my back. The first time I stood up to her my dad slapped me across the face for talking back to my mom. My dad thinks mom is saint. He doesn't know what she has done to me. My mom says if I ever do tell him I would be kicked out. Preston doesn't know that my mom does these thing but whenever he sees a new bruise on my cheek he asks whats wrong. I say the same thing every time." Nothing that concerns you." Preston and I are still close but not as close as we were as children. I stopped cutting when I started cheerleading because I couldn't wear a hoodie over my uniform. This was the first time I cut in a few years. I don't know what happened to make my mom hate me so much but she does. So I just live with it.

I walked down the street towards Mark's house because that is the only other place that could offer me comfort after I totally screwed up with Jason.

He probably hates me and I don't blame him.

I betrayed him.

I want to see if Preston is okay.

Maybe I should go to the hospital first.

Yeah that's what I am going to do.

At least I can see him before I run away.

I can also tell him goodbye.

I walked down the street that lead to the hospital. When I got there I was sweating because even though it is fall, we are in Louisiana were its still summer in the winter.

I went up to the reception desk.

"Hi I am here for Preston Watts." I say and the nurse looks at me.

"Who are you to him?" She asks skeptically.

"Ashley Wild his sister." I say my last name because I know she won't believe me because me and Preston look nothing alike.

"Do you have an ID showing you are who you say you are?" She asks and she has a smug smile saying that she doesn't believe me. I give her a sweet smile and then get my backpack of my back and pull out my school ID. I give her the ID with a glare.

Her smile drops immediately.

"Room 234." She says with a sigh.

"Thank you." I say and then grab my ID and then head to the second floor.

When I get to the room I see him laying there and my parents are gone.

Thank God I don't want to face them and having them asking questions.

I drop my bags by the door way and go by him.

I push his hair out of face and then pull a chair next to his bed.

He looks so pale. There are tubes sticking out of arm and his chest is going up and down.

I hope that it stays that way.

"Preston I'm sorry. This was all my fault. You were probably looking for me because you knew I was gone and that mom and dad wouldn't go find me. That just how great of a brother you are. I wish that I would have been more careful and actually not get kidnapped. I'm sorry for being so secretive but if I tell you it will hurt you and me and I just can't do it. I love you. And Goodbye." I say and then I get up with tears in my eyes and kiss his forehead.

Then I hear the most frightening sound.

Flat line.

-chapter 14-

Bailey's p.o.v

I stood there with Claire looking at me.

Shit. That's all I thought.

I forgot to put my contacts in.

I forgot to put my contacts in.

FML.

Claire took my face and squeezed my cheeks and looked directly in my eyes.

"Why the hell are your EYES RED?" Claire's voice rose and Edgar, Mark's dad, stood up and came up to me. He stood behind Claire glaring at me and Daniel. I felt Daniel tensing behind me.

"Son what have you done?" Edgar said.

I was out of my trance in a second.

"What do you mean 'what he has done,' he didn't do anything! He didn't do this to me! Some stupid vampire that I can't even remember did this to me! He is the one who saved me. The bullshit story about how we meet wasn't real! I was cornered into an alley by a rogue vampire. I haven't shifted then and the vampire turned me! Probably some sick plan or he didn't mean to but he did. I was going to die but Daniel found me and strengthen me. He saved my life!"

After my outburst Daniel was staring down almost.....guilty.

"That's what happened right?" I said looking at Daniel and then at Mark who was looking down at his food.

"Again. What did you do Daniel?" Edgar asked.

"Why do you keep thinking that he did this?" I said turning to look at Edgar and glaring.

"Because only royals vampires or coven leaders can turn people. That is why there is not a lot of vampires in the world! And the place that you got turned was by the castle and there were no vampires who could have turned you except for us!" He shouted in my face.

"No that isn't true. Daniel wouldn't do that." I said backing up shaking my head in disapproval and then looking at Daniel and he was looking down guilty.

"Plus if regular vampire tried to turn you. You would have died." He said with a smirk knowing that he just won this argument.

I didn't stay after that. I left and I didn't come back.

======

Daniel's p.o.v

Guilt.

Guilt.

Guilt.

That is all that I felt.

I watched as Bailey ran from the house.

I turned towards my father and he still had that satisfied smirk on his face but my mom she looked royally pissed off and that was directed towards me.

"You created a monster." My mom said glaring at me.

"You created something that could destroy ALL of us. If she wanted she can try to overt throw me....over throw your dad..... she can kill all of us. And it's all your fault." She said and then she zoomed off out of the house.

I turned towards my dad.

"You son just created two monsters. And this isn't going to end pretty." He said before zooming out himself.

I stood there for a while. Mark finally looked at me. He had a solemn look in his eyes.

"What are we going to do?" He asked running his hands through his hair and leaning back in his chair.

"I have no idea brother."

"She's going to hate you."

"That's what I am afraid of." I said.

Bailey's p.o.v

I ran until I didn't know where I was.

I was in the middle of the woods and I felt the tears run down my cheek and I didn't know how to make it stop. I knelt down and I felt a presence behind me.

Mate. My wolf chanted. I barely hear my wolf and now she wants to show up?

Okay I see how it is.

"What are you doing here?" I ask looking up at him.

"I was about to ask you the same thing." He said and then sat down against the tree beside me.

"Well I asked you first." I said and he sighed.

"My life is so fucked up right now," he said chuckling darkly.

"But it's not as fucked up as mine." I said and then nudged his shoulder.

I felt sparks and I knew that he felt them too because he shivered.

"Well let's just say I found out that my mom and my dad were never really mates and then when my mom did find her mate my dad caught them and my dad killed him and my dad became rogue. Then when I come back here after being kidnapped by my dad I find out that my girlfriend cheated on me with my best friend." He said and then sighed and put his head in his hands.

I didn't know what to say.

I looked at him and his shoulders where shaking indication that he was crying.

I took his head and put it on my lap and stroked his hair and then cooed things in his ears. I felt tingles whenever I touch him but I wanted to comfort him.

After a little while he sat up and then gave me a small smile.

"That's way worse then what I have to go through. I am so sorry."I said and then rested my head on my knees and looked at him. He was looking at me and then all of sudden he started leaning in.

Then in that moment it was just me and him and none of our problems.

Then our lips met and there was just fireworks.

Daniel could never compare to him.

Daniel.

I pulled away and he still had his eyes closed and then he leaned back.

"Wow." He said and leaned back on the tree.

"Yeah that was great but I am with Daniel." I said and then looked at him and he had his jaw clenched and he let out a growl.

"But.....but.... I am your mate." He said and then looked at me with sadness in his eyes.

"I'm sorry but I just got back with him and I love him." But when I said that I felt a huge weight on my shoulders.

Do I love him?

"For how long?" he asked looking at me.

"20 years." I said.

"20 years? How old are you? When did you even meet Daniel? Why have I never seen him?" he asked.

"That's thing I don't know if what I am about to tell you is true or not but here it goes. I meet Daniel when I was 15 in 1995. He saved me from this rogue vampire and from then on I needed blood almost everyday and I didn't age. I was a hybrid and it was because the vampire turned me before I even meet my wolf. Then from then on me and Daniel where the golden couple until about 5 years ago. When he tried to……" I faltered from saying it.

"What did he try to do?" He asked firmly looking me in the eyes.

He looks so concerned.

"He tried to rape me." I said quietly but I know he heard from the loud growl that came from him.

"Yet you still love him?" He asked.

"He apologized and he is trying to prove to me that he is worthy of my apology." I said and he cupped my head in his hands and made me look up at him. He was stroking my cheek and there was tingles going down my cheek and into my heart. My heart started beating faster and I suddenly noticed how close we were.

"He shouldn't have done it in the first place. He should have had the control. He is unworthy of your apology." He said and then I felt his lips on mine again.

I didn't pull away.

But something else did.

or someone.

Let's just say he was PISSED.

====

oh shit's going down in the next chapter.

and ohh we have daniel's p.o.v.

that was an exciting chapter.

let's just say that Ashley's p.o.v will be next because when need to know if Preston is really dead!

or is he going to stay dead?

-chapter 15-

Daniel^^^^

Ashley's p.o.v

I was pushed out of the way as doctors and nurses rushed into the room.

I was pushed out the room and then I came back to my senses.

"NO! Preston you can't leave me!" I was banging on the window that showed Preston's room but I couldn't see anything because they closed the blinds.

"NO! You can't leave me! Please I need you." I was angry.

I was angry at myself for letting him go.

I was angry for being so careless.

I was angry at everything.

At everyone.

Because if he dies. A part of me dies.

I can't lose him.

Mom would find an excuse to make it my fault.

I was slumped against the wall now when the doctor walked out. I stood up.

"Is he okay?" I asked he looked at me with a solemn look.

"We managed to bring him back but we don't know if he will last much longer maybe a day or two." He said.

I slumped to my knees.

I have a day.

One more day with my brother.

One more day with my rock.

My other half.

I got up and walked into his room and sat down on the chair determined to be there when he goes or even if he wakes up.

I will never leave him again.

Jason's p.o.v

Bailey looked at me with fearful eyes.

I knew then that he was behind us.

"What are you doing with MY girlfriend?" He spoke in a dark tone and I choose then to stand up and face him.

"It's funny because she is MY mate." I growled to him.

We were chest to chest and I saw his fist balled and I had mine balled too.

"She doesn't have a mate. She is a new species so she doesn't need one." He said and then walked over to her and grabbed her hand. I let out a deep growl.

"Don't touch her." I said. I can feel my wolf coming to the surface.

"What are you going to do about it pup?" Daniel asked letting go of Bailey's hand and coming towards me.

Just then Bailey became the two of us and pushed us away.

She looked up at Daniel but he was still glaring at me.

"Daniel look at me." She said in a commanding voice.

He instantly looked down.

I knew what she was going to do.

"Daniel I want you to forget that you saw me kissing Jason and you are going to go home and try to talk to your mom." She said and I knew then that she was compelling him. He sped off without another word and she turned to me with a guilty look on her face.

"I can't risk him finding out about us so what I am about to do you might not like." She said and then came up to me and put her hand on my cheek.

I felt the tingles and I put my hand over hers.

"Don't you want to feel this all the time? Don't you want someone who knows when to stop? I can be that person just give me a chance," tears were coming down my face and she looked at me sadly," please don't do this I want to remember."

"I can't." She said and then kissed the tears on my cheeks.

"Please." I said looking in her eyes.

"Jason I don't want you to remember anything after what happened after you left your house. Your wolf took control and you didn't know it till you got lost in the woods." She said and then sped off.

I looked around.

Why do my cheeks tingle?

Where am I?

I sniffed around and smelt her.

If only she she would give me the time of the day.

I started walking back home.

I got home and I went to go find my mom.

I looked in her room and she was fast asleep. I walked up to her and kissed her cheek and then went to my room.

I laid down on my bed and just thought about today.

Something was off.

It was like part of my day was missing.

I didn't even get to see her today.

I fell asleep with Bailey the only the thing I was thinking about.

------- Start here for Today's Part-------

Ashley's p.o.v

The next day....

I didn't want to eat or sleep.

I wanted to wait so I can be there for him.

"Hey Preston. Ummm I don't know what to say but I want you to stay with me please. Just by some miracle you will be able to stay alive. I need you to be here. I need my rock."

I heard someone come in and I saw Mark.

"What are you doing here?" I asked coldly.

"I went to your house to make sure you were okay but your parents said that you ran away and then they told me about Preston so I thought maybe you were here....and well....you are..soo," he looked so nervous while rubbing the back of his neck awkwardly. I looked at his muscles as they flexed.

Focus Ashley.

I looked up at him and he still looked nervous.

I turned towards Preston again and took his hand.

It was still warm so that was a good sign.

I hope.

"What happened?" Mark said sitting on the couch.

"He got into a car accident and he ran into a tree and he didn't have his seat belt on." I said coldly.

It's all your fault.

"He should have had his seat belt on." Mark said bluntly.

I glared at him.

"The reason he didn't have a seat belt on was because he was too busy looking for me since I got kidnapped. IT"S MY FAULT THAT HE IS

LIKE THIS! he WAS LOOKING FOR ME BECAUSE MY STUPID PARENTS DON'T GIVE A SHIT ABOUT ME AND HE KNEW THAT THEY WOULDN'T LOOK FOR ME!" I feel to the ground in sobs and then I felt Mark pick me up.

I felt tingles ALL over.

He put me on his lap and started cooing in my ear and stroking my hair.

I just kept sobbing into his chest even though I knew that him and me wouldn't work out as mates.

We hated each other.

Ever since I heard about what happened to the mermaid king and queen.

What the vampires did to them.

When I realized that Mark was a vampire my freshman year, I instantly hated him and he hated me back.

IF we ever did talk, we would be arguing.

This needs to stop.

I swiftly got up and got back into the chair by Preston's bed.

Mark was still on the floor and then he quickly got up and went to the couch.

"You and I as mates won't work." I said after a moment of silence.

He glared at me. "So you are rejecting me?"

"Yes." All of a sudden I felt this pain in my chest and I held Preston's hand tighter. Then I felt this flow energy and I blacked out.

-chapter 16-

A shley's p.o.v

The next day....

I didn't want to eat or sleep.

I wanted to wait so I can be there for him.

"Hey Preston. Ummm I don't know what to say but I want you to stay with me please. Just by some miracle you will be able to stay alive. I need you to be here. I need my rock."

I heard someone come in and I saw Mark.

"What are you doing here?" I asked coldly.

"I went to your house to make sure you were okay but your parents said that you ran away and then they told me about Preston so I thought maybe you were here....and well....you are..soo," he looked so nervous while rubbing the back of his neck awkwardly. I looked at his muscles as they flexed.

Focus Ashley.

I looked up at him and he still looked nervous.

I turned towards Preston again and took his hand.

It was still warm so that was a good sign.

I hope.

"What happened?" Mark said sitting on the couch.

"He got into a car accident and he ran into a tree and he didn't have his seat belt on." I said coldly.

It's all your fault.

"He should have had his seat belt on." Mark said bluntly.

I glared at him.

"The reason he didn't have a seat belt on was because he was too busy looking for me since I got kidnapped. IT"S MY FAULT THAT HE IS LIKE THIS! he WAS LOOKING FOR ME BECAUSE MY STUPID PARENTS DON'T GIVE A SHIT ABOUT ME AND HE KNEW THAT THEY WOULDN'T LOOK FOR ME!" I feel to the ground in sobs and then I felt Mark pick me up.

I felt tingles ALL over.

He put me on his lap and started cooing in my ear and stroking my hair.

I just kept sobbing into his chest even though I knew that him and me wouldn't work out as mates.

We hated each other.

Ever since I heard about what happened to the mermaid king and queen.

What the vampires did to them.

When I realized that Mark was a vampire my freshman year, I instantly hated him and he hated me back.

IF we ever did talk, we would be arguing.

This needs to stop.

I swiftly got up and got back into the chair by Preston's bed.

Mark was still on the floor and then he quickly got up and went to the couch.

"You and I as mates won't work." I said after a moment of silence.

He glared at me. "So you are rejecting me?"

"Yes." All of a sudden I felt this pain in my chest and I held Preston's hand tighter. Then I felt this flow energy and I blacked out.

Mark's p.o.v

I rushed to the couch and caught Ashley before she fell to the floor. She had passed out but I had no idea why.

I heard a groan and I looked up and saw a glow coming from Preston.

Then the strangest thing happened.

All his scars were clearing up in the blink of an eye and his skin was starting to grow tanner.

To say I was surprised was an under statement.

Not even vampires could heal that fast and plus they couldn't bring someone back from that close to death.

I looked at the Ashley and she was passed out but she was burning up.

All of a sudden a doctor walked in and saw us.

"What is going on here?" He asked eyeing Ashley and then Preston who was know awake but was totally confused about what happened. "And how is he alive? He only had about two days!" HE said looking astonished.

Stupid people bringing him to a human hospital.

I laid Ashley down on the ground carefully and then walked over to the doctor.

"You are going to leave and forget this patient and everything that happened and you are also going delete or get rid of any evidence that he was at this hospital." I compelled him and he walked off.

I took Ashley in my arms and stood up and then looked Preston who looked fine.

"Can you walk?" I asked.

"Yeah I'm pretty sure." He got up off the bed and then stood to his feet. He stumbled for awhile before finally getting control over his balance.

"Okay let's get out of here."

Preston followed me quickly out of the building so we won't get caught.

We did get caught a few times but I quickly compelled them to forget.

We quickly got outside and we walked to Daniel's car that I borrowed to get here.

I don't even know how Ashley got here. The hospital was about a mile outside of town!

Not very convenient.

I put Ashley in the back and instructed Preston to get to the front.

I got into the front seat and then started driving to Ashley's house.

Shit I don't know where she lives.

"Where do you live?"

"254 Candlewood Dr."

I nodded and then i started going towards there. It was silent until Preston wanted to open his mouth.

"What exactly happened?"

"What do you remember?" I asked looking at him curiously.

"I remember my parents saying that Ashley hadn't been home all day."

"Yeah we were kidnapped by some rogues." I said.

"And then after that I remember getting into the car and going to look for her and to make sure she was okay after that I kinda blacked out." He said sounding confused.

"Well apparently you were in an accident I don't know everything that happened but they said you didn't have your seat belt and that you were supposed to die." I said not leaving out anything.

"It was that bad? Then how am I alive?" He asked.

"I have no idea how you are alive but I think it has to do with something that involves Ashley because right before you magically healed she took your hand and there was this glowing light and then she passed out and then all of your scars were gone and your skin started looking tanner. I have never seen anything like it because not even a vampire can heal that fast." I said as I pulled into there driveway.

He stayed silent while we got out of the car and I went to go get Ashley from the back of the car. Her shirt rose up at her wrists and I saw some fairly new scars on them.

I felt my heart tear a little.

I lifted here gently and then went inside.

"Where should I put her?" I asked.

"Preston?" Someone said from another room and I heard someone start sobbing.

I walked into the room with Ashley still in my hands and saw a women that must be Preston and Ashley's mom because she was sobbing while hugging the life out of Preston.

"Um excuse me?" I asked timidly looking at the parent's of my mates.

"Yes?" The women said and looked at Ashley in my arms and she sighed in relief.

"Oh my gosh thank the lord she is okay." She said and I could hear a hint of sarcasm in her voice and I immediately went into a defensive stance.

"Where can I put her?" I asked trying to hide the anger in my voice.

"And who are you?" The man on the couch said.

"I am Mark and I am a friend of Ashley's." I said not completely trusting them with the mate thing.

"Just go put her in her room go down the hallway the one to the left at the end of the hall." The women said not even asking if her daughter was okay even though she was passed out in my arms before going to hug her son while still sobbing.

"Thanks." I said and then went down to Ashley's room. When I got there I gently put her on her bed and then tucked her in. I kissed her forehead and then went out into the living room and was about to leave but someone had to stand in my way.

"I don't want you near my daughter again because I know what you are and I know what you have done to our people." Ashley's father said standing in front of me and glaring.

I straightened my posture and then looked him directly at him.

"I am sorry but I have no idea what you are talking about because I am just here to help your daughter but apparently you don't care enough about her to actually ask how she is and then try to intimidate me when I can easily snap my fingers and have you killed but I won't because that would make your daughter very angry and I rather not be on her bad side anymore."

"You know what your father did to the mermaid kingdom an-" he started but I cut him off

"I am not my father and I will never be that despicable son of bitch." I said before going around and leaving him.

Great first impressions don't you think?

-chapter 17-

Bailey's p.o.v

I woke up with an arm slung around me.

I turned around and there was Jason.

WAIT WHAT?

I fell out of the bed.

I looked up and saw Daniel looking down at me from the bed.

Wait wasn't that Jason?

"What's wrong?" He asked with his voice husky from just waking up.

I shook my head thinking something was wrong with my head "Yeah I am fine don't worry about me." then gave him a smile to reassure him.

He smiled back and then rolled back on to the bed.

I sighed and then put my hand to my head. I didn't feel warm.

It must be from starting the mate's bond by kissing his cheek.

Ugh Why did I have to do that?

because he is our mate

I sat up immediately because this is the first time I've heard my wolf since I got home.

What was her name again?

Talia and the reason I haven't been talking to you is because I am mad at you for picking that blood sucker over our mate.

She growled the last part.

I love Daniel.

Do you really? Or do you just feel obligated to be with him because you have been with him since like forever and he saved you?

Damn wolf and her good points.

Damn right.

Shut up. I waited a few seconds but I knew she was in the back of my mind.

I got up on my feet and then looked at the bed at Daniel.

Do I love him?

I mean he isn't ugly and he makes me feel safe but something is missing.

He isn't your mate.

I sighed and I knew what I had to do.

=======

Ashley's p.o.v

I woke up in my bed. I looked around wondering how I got here.

Then I remembered everything.

Preston.

I rushed out my room and to the kitchen where I saw Preston sitting at the counter eating cereal.

I ran to him and tackled him into a hug.

He groaned and then laughed.

"Can you please get off of me?" He asked and I slowly got off of him.

"How are you here? How are you not dead? You supposed to be de-" I burst into tears and fell to the ground.

Preston quickly wrapped his arms around me.

"Hey hey shhhh I am here now that's all that matters." He cooed.

"But..but..you got...into..the..car.....to...look...for me and you could..... have...died...beCAUSE...OF....ME!" I said in hysterics by the end of my dragging sentence.

"No Ashley it isn't your fault. I choose to get in that car and not put my seat belt on and it's also the guy's fault for swerving on the road on his phone." He said still rubbing my back.

"It is m-"

"NO!" He said and then took my face in his hands."It is NOT YOUR FAULT! IN no way is it your fault." He said kissing my forehead. I snuggled into him and finally stopped crying but just wanted to be hold by my brother.

After a few more minutes my mom(A/N Bitch alert) walked in.

"Ashley can I speak with you in my office?" She asked looking kinda pissed off.

This can't be good.

I nodded and then got up and followed her to her office.

I walked in in front of her and she came after me closing the door.

"Sit. NOW!" She said and I quickly sat on the couch and she came in front of me and paced.

She did that for a few minutes before reaching out and slapping me on the face.

I held my hand on my cheek where I can feel some tear drops start to come down.

"How dare you bring that creature in this house when you know what his family did to our kingdom! I thought you were smarter than that! Apparently not."

"What are you talking about?" suddenly getting angry and standing up ad glaring at her.

She matched my stance and then glared harder at me.

"Mark. That is what I am talking about. Apparently he is your friend and he is a vampire for god's sakes! What is wrong with you! He even threatened your father!" She said.

"We aren't friends. We are mates!" I screamed at her and her face went pale.

"what?" She shrieked.

"I am going to reject him anyway because we would never work." I said and sat back down on the couch.

"Damn right or else I am pulling you out of cheer leading." She said sternly.

"You can't do that!" I screamed at her and I felt myself get angry again.

"You will reject him and then also we are moving away from this town." She said and then went to leave but I grabbed her hand I felt this power coursing through me.

"Listen mother," I said mother with enough in my venom," stop being a little bitch and let us stay here I will avoid him just let us stay here." I said looking right in her eyes.

"No. You don't have a say in this house." She said and then took her arm out of my grasp. She kept trying to walk out.

I felt this energy and then I blacked out.

Why does this keep happening?

-chapter 18-

Mark's p.o.v

I got home after dropping off Ashley and walked in to the golden couple making out on the couch.

"Get a room." I said and they immediately sprang apart.

"Hey little bro what's wrong you looked pissed." Daniel stated bluntly and I gave him the middle finger.

"I met Ashley's parents and-"

"Wow that was quick but I thought she rejected you?" Daniel interrupted.

"Yes she did reject me but she ran away from home so I went to the hospital were her brother's was at and anyway he's fine by the way," noticing Bailey's concerning face," He was supposed to die but Ashley saved him some how." I said and then sat down the chair across from the couch in the living room.

"How?" Bailey asked.

"I don't know all I know is that Ashley started crying about Preston and she was also mad at me for some odd reason and then this light shone and

Ashley passed out and Preston started healing in front of our eyes. Faster than even a vampire can do." I said rubbing my forehead suddenly getting a headache from all this commotion.

"That's strange." Bailey said.

"For real." Daniel said.

"Don't say that it doesn't suit you." Bailey said scrunching her eyebrows together.

Daniel just laughed and kissed her forehead. I groaned and got up and went to my room hoping to get some well needed sleep.

I woke up to my cell phone ringing. I looked at the time and it said it was already noon.

"Hello?" I asked not even looking at the caller id.

"Hey Mark this is Preston something happened with Ashley and-"

"I'm on my way." I said before springing up and leaving but Bailey stopped me on my way out.

"Mark can I talk to you?" She asked looking a little desperate.

"I need to go see Ashley." I said

"What? Why? Can I come?"

I groaned and then nodded and we headed towards Ashley's house.

=====

When we got there Preston was waiting outside.

"Hey Bailey, Mark." Preston said and then led us inside.

Ashley was on the couch passed out again.

I groaned.

I have been doing that a lot lately.

"What happened?" I asked.

"I don't know but Ashley went to go talk to our mom in our office and then I see this glowing light and I ran in there to see Ashley and my mom passed out on the floor." Preston said looking worriedly at Ashley.

"Where is your mom?" I asked looking around for her but she wasn't here.

"My dad took her to the hospital because her heart rate was slow but he has to leave for a business trip soon so I will go there and I need you to stay here with Ashley." Preston explained.

"Okay fine." I said after thinking through it.

"Thanks." Preston said before heading out the door.

"Wear a seat belt!" I called out and he flipped me the bird before closing the door.

I pulled up a chair next to the couch and took Ashley's hand in mine.

It just felt so right.

But we can't be together.

"Hey Mark?" Bailey asked grabbing another chair and pulling it next to mine.

"Yeah?" I said looking at her and she looked so sad.

"What was Daniel like when I left?" She asked.

"He was a monster. He turned off his feelings and he didn't give a crap bout anyone except for himself." I said.

"Oh." Was all she said before we went into a silence. It wasn't an awkward silence, but silence of people trying to think things through.

Why does this keep happening to Ashley?

Is she a hybrid like Bailey, too?

No way her mom and dad are both mermaids.

Unless her mother was being unfaithful but with what kind of creature?

No other creatures are more powerful healers than vampires.

Unless.

No it can't be them they are extinct.

So what is it?

===========

Bailey's p.o.v

Maybe if I break it to him gently he will not go back to the way he is.

or will he?

Then the door bell rang.

I got up and answered it and who was there made my heart swell.

=============

Jason's p.o.v (it has been too long)

All I have been thinking about is Bailey.

Just her.

My chest gets heavier every time I think about her because I picture her with him.

I kept having this dream that I was talking to her and just bonding with her but then he shows up.

It was a nightmare.

Today I finally decided that I should go see her.

I went to her house but her mom said she was at Mark's house and that means she is with him.

So I headed to a house that I swore I would never go to after finding out what happened.

There wasn't cars in the driveway but I still rang the doorbell and who greeted made my chest hurt.

"Hey Jason." Bailey said smiling at me.

"Hey." I said wearing a grin that I haven't been wearing the last few days.

"Come in we have some things to talk about." She said and then lead me into the house and to the living room where I saw Mark holding Ashley's hand while Ashley laid passed out on the couch.

"What happened?" I asked looking at Ashley concerned.

"Same thing that happened when we were in the prison. She passed out after using whatever power she has inside of her." Mark said.

"Do you know where this power is coming from and why it's just showing up?" I asked.

"I think it started when she reconized Mark as her mate." Bailey said.

"That is true she only used her powers AFTER she find out I was her mate so that could be a possibility." Mark said.

"But where does this power come from?" I asked.

"I think either her mother had an affair." Mark said.

"But that would mean Preston is hybrid along with Ashley and he hasn't shown any signs of being anything but a mermaid," I said ," With Ashley I remember when she got really angry her eyes would glow a dark blue." I said now really thinking about it.

"And I have gotten Preston mad once and nothing happened with his eyes." Mark said.

"Maybe she isn't even their daughter." Bailey said.

"That's a possibility but it is unlikely because they are the only few mermaids that are alive." Mark said.

"That's right the vampires killed most of the mermaid population after they posed a supposed threat to them." Bailey scoffed.

"Yeah my father is crazy." Mark said.

"Yeah and now they know I am hybrid too so I have no idea what they are going to do with me."Bailey said looking scared. All I wanted to do was take her in my arms and comfort her but she is with someone else so I restrained myself and my wolf.

"Hey Jason can I talk with you in private?" Bailey asked. I perked up and then nodded.

We headed to the backyard where they had a table and we sat there.

"Um I don't know how to start but...um I think I am going to break up with Daniel." She said.

"Really?" I asked a little unsure because I know that she loves him.

"Really." She said.

"But why?" I asked.

She sighed,"I think I stopped loving him when he tried to rape me because no one who loves me should do that to me and-"

"Damn right." She gave me a look and put my hands up in surrender.

"Anyway and then when he came save us I thought that I still loved but then I realized that I only loved what he did. I loved that he came saved us and how nice he was." She said, "But i can never love him again like I used to because he lost my love when he did that to me. He lost my trust in him."

"So what does that have do with me?" I asked a little timidly.

"It means that I want to give this mate thing a chance." She said and my wolf howled in joy.

"Okay that's absolutely okay with me."

"But I still need to break the news to Daniel so just give me a couple of days." She said and she stood up and then sat on my lap. I gave her a peck on the cheek.

"I can get used to this." I said feeling tingles all over.

" I know but I have to go inside now to check on Ashley." She said and then got off my lap and headed inside.

I stood up and did a little happy dance and then walked inside but the scene that greeted me was not what I expected.

Then I felt a cloth go over my mouth and I passed out.

-chapter 19-

Mark's p.o.v

I already knew who took us this time because I woke up in the room that I grew up.

In the castle.

Shit. I knew that they would come for us.

I sat up in my bed and the headed downstairs and to the living room where I saw Jason, Bailey, and Ashley sitting down.

"What are we doing here?" I asked.

"Well your mom and dad kidnapped us." Ashley said bluntly and looking a little pissed.

"Also I have this gigantic ring on a finger that I don't know where it came from!" Bailey exclaimed.

"Well that is my ring of course." Daniel said entering the room from the other doorway.

"What do you mean it is your?" Jason said standing up and glaring at Daniel.

"Well since little Bailey was going to leave me for you, little wolf, I kidnapped her and brought her here to where she will marry me and I shall become king." Daniel said.

"I will not marry you!" Bailey said trying to take the ring off but failing.

"Tsk tsk Bailey you can't take that ring of because a witch put a spell on it making me the only one to take it off of you which isn't going to happen." Daniel said smirking thinking he has won.

Then I saw it.

The familiar coldness in his eyes.

He turned off his emotions.

"Again really Daniel?" I asked and Daniel shrugged.

"Where did you get a witch from anyway they hide themselves from supernaturals like us." Ashley said.

"Well mom and dad have one and they let me borrow her and that's how I got the ring." Daniel said.

"Hold on a minute the only reason you want to marry me is because you want to be king?" Bailey asked finally digesting all the Daniel told her.

"Yes little naive little Bailey. That's the only reason I ever dated you in the first place just for the power." Daniel said but I knew that wasn't true. He only is saying that because he has his emotions off.

"Bullshit." Bailey said catching on to what I see.

"Nope." Daniel said popping the 'p'. Bailey went up and slapped him and leaving a scar where her ring scratched him but it quickly healed.

"Looks like I am going to lock you up until our wedding." Daniel said grabbing Bailey's wrist before she can slap him again. Jason looked ready to explode.

"Get your hands off of her." He growled and I knew his wolf was on the edge.

Daniel let go but he smirked.

"You little wolf I have a special job for you." Daniel said before going over to him and injecting him with wolfs bane with vampire speed.

Bailey screamed and went over to him where he was crouched down.

"Are you okay?" She asked looking him in the face.

"Yeah he just suppressed my wolf." Jason said.

"How did you even find out about them?" I asked.

"Well darling brother. I came to Ashley house but you were to caught up in your mind to notice and walked to the back where I heard voices and I heard Bailey's confession so vampire speed back home and got what I needed and kidnapped all of you because if I would have left any of you. you would have came save Bailey and there is no one else there to save you." Daniel said smirking and then he took Jason by the ear and dragged him out with Bailey following them.

I looked at Ashley and she was deep in thought. I went to go sit next to her.

"Hey are you okay?" I said bringing my hand up and stroking her cheek and she flinched so I put my hand down.

"No there is something going on with me and then we keep getting kidnapped." Ashley sighed and then turned towards me and looked me in my eyes.

"I want to try this mates thing out." She said and my eyes widened in shock.

"What? Why? What about your parents and-" She shut me up by placing her lips on mine.

It was amazing.

Our lips started moving in sync and I deepened the kiss but then she pulled away.

"That's a good way to shut me up." I said and then pecked her on the lips.

She giggled.

"But really what changed your mind?" I asked.

"Well I haven't had the best life and I get a mate which is one of the best things you could get and I just flat out reject him without giving him a chance because I was basing him on his father which doesn't justify what kind of person he is. My mate is someone who was there for me and I am glad he was." She said with a smile and I gave her a smile back and then I kissed her.

"Aww who is this sweetie?" Said a voice that is all too familiar.

"Mom this is Ashley my mate." I said.

=====

Bailey's p.o.v

"Where are you taking him?" I said running behind Daniel who was dragging Jason by the ear.

"To the servants quarter were he will get dressed and be my servant for the rest of his pathetic life." Daniel spat.

"No! You can't do that!" I shouted at him.

"Watch me." He said and then vampire sped away to where I couldn't follow him.

I stomped my foot and the turned around only to be greeted by a woman. She was really skinny and dull black hair and had green eyes and she looked undernourished.

"Ahh so you are the girl that I had to make the ring for." She said

"uhhh... yeah your the witch?" I asked.

She laughed,"My names Sandra and I am also the one who made a barrier around the house so no one can exit after coming in so you and your friends are stuck here." She said.

"But why? We didn't do anything to you"

"Yes I know but what Daniel would have done to me would land me in the bottom of the ocean." She said.

"I'm so sorry you are probably forced to be here."

"I have been here my whole life since I was a baby and the queen ordered people to steal me from my mother." She said sadly.

"How old are you?"

"45" She said but she still looked 25 even with no food in her system.

"When is the last time you ate?"

"About two weeks" She said sadly.

"Well come with me and I am going to get you some food." I said and before she could object I vampire sped to the kitchen.

I'm glad I remember where it is or else that would have been embarrassing.

I sat her down and then started getting a bowl and then some cereal out.

Trust me don't ever let me cook.

I am horrible at it.

"Cereal?" She asked looking at the bowl skeptically.

"I can't cook but that doesn't mean I can't give you food. Now what type of cereal do you want?"

"I always liked frosted flakes." She said timidly.

"Okay." I said and then poured her a bowl of cereal.

When she took her first bite her hair started growing fuller and her skin became smoother.

"What? B-but how?" I stuttered looking at a completely different woman in front of me.

"You don't know much about witches don't you?"

I shook my head no.

She laughed," Well when witches aren't fed probably they wrinkle their skin and make their hair dull and make themselves look skinnier to make people feel bad and give them food. And it works most of the time." she said.

"Wow. That's awesome." I said.

"What are you doing?" Daniel boomed followed by Jason in a servant's outfit.

Damn he looked good in tux.

Focus Bailey.

"I gave her food because she hasn't been fed properly." I said crossing my arms over my chest and glaring at him.

He came up and tried to slap me but his hand froze in mid air.

I looked over and Sandra looked pissed.

"You shall never touch a woman in that way." She boomed.

She let his hand go and he glared at her and then went up to her and slit her throat killing her.

I gasped.

"What the actual fuck?" I asked getting angry.

"She was in my way of disciplining my fiance." He said and then came back to me but I was angry and stopped his hand mid way. I can feel my wolf coming to the surface.

"Don't you dare touch me that way." I compelled him.

He slowly put his hand down.

"Good now go away. I want to talk to Jason." I said and he nodded then walked out.

"Why didn't you compel him to take the ring off?" He asked.

"Because even if I got the ring off, we are still stuck her because Sandra put a spell on the castle so no one can get out." I sighed. I looked at Jason and then wrapped my arms around him.

"Why can't life be simple?" I asked.

"Because we aren't simple people." He said and then kissed my forehead.

"You know with every force field there is a weak spot," Mark said coming in with Ashley by his side," We just have to find it."

"Okay tomorrow we find that weak spot and I will compel Daniel to take this stupid ring off and we will be gone."

"But we will just find you again." Claire said coming in with Enzo.

"If you really want to come up with an escape plan you might want to do it in a soundproof room," Enzo said, " Also you won't be leaving this castle because right now Bailey and Ashley you under arrest for being too powerful."Enzo said and then guards came in and tried to take me but I quickly turned into my wolf and fought them off along with guards trying to take Ashley.

"Stay away" I growled but then I felt a needle go in my back and I looked up and saw Daniel.

'Bastard' I thought before blacking out.

-chapter 20-

Daniel's p.o.v

She really thought she could go along with her little escape plan.

That's why I am dragging her big ass wolf to the cellar along with Ashley and Jason.

I don't know what is going on with that Ashley chick but she is too powerful and she needs to be terminated.

But Mark might hate us forever.

Who gives a shit? He already hates me.

I dragged her to one of our 'special' cells and locked her in. Shows her right for trying to escape. When we get married in three days I will make sure to mark her and make her my little sex slave.

Just thinking about her under me gives me a boner.

I shook it off and then passes the other cells with the others and I looked into the one with Jason.

Little Bastard.

Should have killed him the minute I saw him touching her.

I growled and then left.

I went upstairs into my dad's office where my mom and dad were.

"So what's the plan?" I asked laying down on their couch in there.

"Ashley will be executed in two days and then you will marry Bailey the third day and then get the throne on the fourth day." Dad said but it sounded forced.

"Are you sure about that?" I asked raising an eyebrow at him.

"Of course." He said and then gestured me to leave.

"Whatever." I said and then went back down to the cellars to see if she was up yet.

I got down there and Ashley was awake and her eyes were glowing dark blue.

"Stupid vampires thinking you can lock me up." She said before bursting the cell door down and then coming for me she had me by my neck and pinned me to the wall.

"I'll have fun killing you." She said and was about to kill me but a voice stopped her.

"Ashley don't do that he is still my brother." Mark said.

But he hates me.

"Fine" and she let go off me not before punching me in the head and knocking me out.

Mark's p.o.v

"Can you let me out now?" I asked and she came over and just grabbed the bars and tore them of. I ran to her and then kissed her. She kissed back and I broke the kiss and looked at her and her eyes were back to normal.

"Good because you scary when your eyes are like that." I said and she giggled.

"Can you maybe get us out now?" Bailey said. Ashley looked back and Bailey was at her cell door smirking at us.

"Of course." Ashley said blushing a little.

She quickly took the cell door and flung it off and Bailey came out and Ashley moved to Jason's cell but he was still passed out.

"I know how to wake him." Bailey and then went in after Ashley ripped the door off.

=====

Jason's p.o.v

I woke up to lips on mine,

I know these lips so I kissed her back and I felt her smile in the kiss and she pulled away.

It was amazing.

"Wow. Wish I can wake up to that everyday."

"Keep it up and maybe you will." Bailey said and then stood up and offered me her hand.

I got up and looked around and saw that we were in a cell.

"What did I miss?" I asked.

"Just me being a bad ass." Ashley said smiling.

Mark and Bailey laughed but I was still a little confused.

"Don't worry about it." Bailey said kissing my cheek and I kissed hers back.

"Ew get a room." Mark said.

"No No mister I am not the one who suddenly started making out with my mate in the middle of the hallway." Bailey said waging her finger at them and Ashley blushed.

"Okay let's go." Mark said.

"We still can't leave because we still need to find the weak spot AND I still need to get this ring off." Bailey said putting her hand up showing us the ring.

"Also we have my mom and dad to deal with." Mark said.

"I think I have something to persuade them that we aren't a threat." Ashley said looking excited.

"What?" Bailey asked and Ashley leaned over and whispered something in her ear and Bailey nodded.

"That sound perfect." Bailey said.

"What?" Me and Mark asked.

"You'll see." Bailey said.

======

Ashley's p.o.v

This is one of the best ideas I have ever had.

We went upstairs and went into the office of Enzo.

He immediately stood up and coming towards us.

"Hold on we have a proposition for you." I said putting my hand up.

"You are to be killed in two days and you Bailey are going to be married in three days no argument needed." Claire said crossing her arms.

"Just her us out please?" Bailey said and then gestured Mark and Jason to the couch to her what we have planned to.

"Okay you have tow minutes." Claire said sitting down on Enzo's desk and Enzo nodded his head.

"We thought that maybe you can use us as a weapon." I started.

Claire and Enzo glared at us.

"How so?" Enzo said.

"Well you can let us go and in exchange we will fight with you in any battles. We can be like your secret weapon all you have to do is give us a call and we will be there to help y'all out." I said.

"We can even be an intimidation kind of thing like we can intimidate people to agree with any plans you have." Bailey added.

Enzo and Clarie were deep in thought and then Enzo nodded his head and then so did Claire.

Me and Bailey up and down and hugged each other knowing we just got out of being killed.

'I like it," Jason said, " as long as you are alive." Coming up and giving Bailey a hug.

"I like it too." Mark said coming to me and kissing me on the cheek.

"Y'all are too cute. Now there is one problem." Claire said.

"Me." Daniel said standing in the doorway looking pissed.

"Son." Enzo said getting up but before he can say anything else Daniel had me pinned into the wall and had his fangs on my neck.

"I wonder what hybrid blood tastes like." He said before biting into my neck.

I hurt like hell.

Then I felt him loosen his grip and he fell down on the ground and I slid down the wall feeling dizzy.

==========

Mark's p.o.v

All I saw was red when I heard Ashley scream next thing I know I am crushing Daniel's heart and him dying.

He fell to the ground and Ashley slid down the wall on the brink of unconscious.

I just killed my brother.

I heard gasps and then my mother say "Serves him right."

I turned to her and she just shrugged.

"He messed with someone's mate I would kill him too." She said.

I turned around and Bailey was pale. She then ran out of the room and Jason was following her.

I dropped to my knees.

I just killed my brother.

========

Bailey's p.o.v

I ran out the room and to the nearest bathroom. I slumped down near the toilet and vomited.

He's dead.

Daniel's gone.

My first love is gone.

I heard someone knock on the door and yelling at me but I couldn't hear what they were saying and then I heard a slam and then someone picked me up.

I felt tingles all over so I knew it was Jason.

He set me on his lap and rocked me and cooed in my ear sweet nothings.

He's gone.

Ashley's p.o.v

Mark picked me up and took me to a bedroom.

By the scent everywhere I knew it was his room.

He laid me down on the bed.

"Are you okay?" I asked Mark. I looked up at him and he looked so sad and pale.

He just shook his head no so I scooted over and told him to come lay with me. He slowly got on the bed with me and laid his head on my chest and just cried.

I cooed sweet nothings to him knowing he just needed comfort right now.

-chapter 21-

A/N Last Chapter

2 weeks later.....

Bailey's p.o.v

"Okay children be careful!" Claire said giving us all hugs.

These past two weeks have been rough.

The funeral was the hardest but I think we are all accepting it now.

Claire started trusting me and Ashley more and we have special phones so she can contact us when she needs us.

She also brought a witch to take away the stupid entering and exiting spell and that took a week because the witch had to find the source and stupid stuff like that.

"Bye Claire. Just call when needed." After another 15 minutes we were all in cars on the way home.

I was in the car with Ashley because we live by each other and Jason and Mark where in the other.

"I bet my mom is totally pissed right now." I said.

"My mom probably doesn't even care." Ashley said looking down and shrugging.

"Hey she's your mom she loves you, you know?" I said rubbing her shoulder but she looked up at me with absolute sadness in her eyes.

"We have been getting closer this past few weeks and I wanted to tell you something." She said and then taking in some.

"My mom abuses me. Every time I do something wrong or if she is just angry she'd slap me." Ashley said. " There was this one time that I accidentally but my finger while chopping vegetables and she slapped me for getting blood on the vegetables and ruining the whole meal." She said and then she busted out crying and I took her and gave her a tight.

"I never did anything wrong. I was always a good child she just doesn't love me." She said.

"I'm so sorry you had to go through that." I said not sure what to say.

"I still go through it." She said.

I just kept holding her while she cried and soon enough we pulled up to my house.

"I have to go but call me if you just need to escape that okay?" I said, she nodded and then I closed the door and headed to my house.

I didn't know what to do so I knocked because I haven't been here in a while.

My mom opened up and when she saw me she pulled me into a hug and started crying.

"I'm sorry. I was kidnapped. Again. This is a long story so maybe we should go inside to tell it." I said.

"Don't ever do that to me again!" She said bu then we went inside were I proceed to tell her what happened.

==========

Mark's p.o.v

The car ride I slept most of the time.

By the time we got home they already dropped of Jason. I got out the car and went into my house.

Now my life was back to normal.

But I have a wonderful mate to go along with it.

============

Ashley's p.o.v

I got home and Preston's car was in the driveway but my parent's weren't.

I went inside and immediately got tackled into a hug by Preston.

"Where have you've been I have been worried sick!" He said now looking pretty mad.

"You sound like a mom." I said chuckling.

"Well mom is still in the hospital." Preston said.

"What why?" I asked surprised she is still there,

"She is in a coma and they don't now when she will wake up." Preston said sadly.

"Can you drive me to the hospital. I can heal her." I said and Preston nodded his head and we headed to the car.

====

When we got to the hospital room that my mom was in I quickly ran over to her and took her hand.

I tried to focus any energy that I had in me and healed her and all of a sudden a light glowed from my hand and her eyes opened.

I looked at her but when she saw me she glared.

"This is all you fault!" She screamed.

"I know and I am so sorry I didn't mean for that to happen." I said starting to cry because I realized this was my fault.

All my fault.

"I should have never taken you but of course a promise is a promise." She said to herself.

"What do you mean?"

"Look you little bitch," She said coldly," You aren't my daughter but I promised your mother that I would take care of you so I did but now you caused me be in a come for however long! So right now I think I have the right to tell you. You aren't my daughter and never were your mother had an affair with someone that I never knew and when your father found out he went mad. He threatened every type of supernatural being and that was a big mistake on his part. Anyway the vampires took the threat seriously and they killed them but before they killed your mother she told me to take you and take care of. I promised but know you have caused all this trouble. I don't care as long as I keep my family safe and that is why I am kicking you out."

I was in shock.

I wasn't her daughter.

"Who was mom and dad?"

" The mermaid king and queen." She said.

=============

Jason's p.o.v

I got out of the car to my house and went into my house.

My mom was sitting on the couch but something was different.

There were bags packed and pictures were taken down of the wall.

"Finally you are home! Where have you've been? I have been worried sick!" She said and then came give me a hug.

"Why are all these bags packed?" I asked confused.

"I have done something horrible and we need to leave before they the police come find us." She said and then started taking some bags and going outside and putting them in the trunk of the car.

"Where are we going?" I asked a little worried I have to leave Bailey.

"You'll see but we need to go!" She said and kept going so fast.

"Wait! Stop!" I said grabbing her arm.

"What did you do?" I asked.

"Eric came here and he told me that he wanted a divorce and that he was cheating on me and stiff and blah blah and then he wanted the house and kept saying that he wanted to take you and how I was an unfit parent so I kinda wolfed out on him and killed him." She said with tears in her eyes.

I pulled her into hug. "She it's okay where is he buried?" I asked.

"Far out in the woods but you know joggers and their ability to find dead bodies and that is why we need to leave." She said.

I nodded.

I will just come visit Bailey when I can.

========

When we got to the airport and found out where we were going I turned towards my mom.

"No I can't go!" I said and started walking away. My mom grabbed my arm.

"You have to go or else the police will find out about us and supernaturals."

I thought about it and then nodded sadly.

When we got onto the plane and we were about to take off I said the words I thought I would never have to say.

I Jason Clause reject Bailey Wild as my mate.

==========

Bailey's p.o.v

I sat up in my bed with the words imprinted in my mind.

Why?

Why is he rejecting me?

What did I do?

I screamed out in pain and my mom came in and started rocking me while I cried in her arms.

"He rejected me." I said sadly.

========

The next week goes on so slow before Ashley busts into my room and makes me get up.

"Jesus you smell like death and that's bad since I am mates with a vampire."

"Don't mention mates in front of me." I said sadly.

Ashley rolled her eyes.

"Go take a shower and get dressed and come down stairs." She said with a tone with no argument in her voice so I listened to her and showered and dressed and went into the living room.

"There's the zombie." Said Mark sitting on the couch. I just flipped him the bird.

"Why am I up?" I asked looking at Ashley and sitting down on one of the chairs.

She smiled,"We are going out and making you feel better," She said determined.

"I just want the pain to go away."I said and curled up into a ball on the chair that I was sitting on.

"You could just turn off your emotions." Mark said then Ashley hit him on the shoulder and shook her head at him.

That sounds pretty promising.

So I focused on one emotion: anger.

Then I turned my emotions off.

I suddenly looked up and felt determined so I got my shoes on and head to his house.

"Where are you going?" Ashley said coming to stop me.

"I am going to find that son of a bitch." I said before slamming the door shut and setting out on my journey.

Jason Clause you better watch out because I'm coming for you.

THE END

www.ingramcontent.com/pod-product-compliance
Lightning Source LLC
Chambersburg PA
CBHW072210070526
44585CB00015B/1280